Reach for the Counter,
Not for the Stars

Reach for the Counter, Not for the Stars

A Weekly Devotional for Finding Humor,
Beauty, and Grace in the Ordinary Days

RICHARD J. DANIELS

Stonebrook Publishing
Saint Louis, Missouri

A STONEBROOK PUBLISHING BOOK
©2025 Richard J. Daniels

Library of Congress Control Number: 2025917159

ISBN: 978-1-955711-42-5

This luminous collection of weekly devotionals is a lifeline for every mother who's ever wondered if the endless carousel of laundry, lunch-packing, and late-night rocking chairs could hold more than exhaustion. Packed with both humor and wisdom, these pages invite you to see the beauty tucked inside the ordinary. With every reading, you'll feel encouraged to embrace the mundane as a gift, to trade frustration for perspective, and to rest in the grace that covers both the moments we get right and the ones we don't. Do yourself a favor and enjoy this uplifting guide that celebrates the resilience, grace, and love woven through the journey of motherhood.

—**Heather G. Johnson**
Mother, Realtor, Cyclist

It's so easy to get caught up in striving to excel and doing everything right to ensure positive outcomes for ourselves and our families day after day after day. How wonderful to be reminded that there is joy in life's simpler tasks! To find grace and purpose—and even pleasure—in everyday things is the gift. What a beautiful reminder to appreciate the moment and our purpose to serve those we love without expectation!

—**Patricia M. Hogan**
Mother, Realtor, Keeper of Family Traditions

For my sister, Patty—
For always putting family and faith first
with grace, humor, and humility.

To our mother, Sheila—
Who instilled that same spirit in both of us, our three
brothers, and all our children.

And to my wife, Meg, who already knows and lives her
faith and makes everyone feel like they are enough.
You are a GEM.

This devotional journey is for every soul learning to reach
for the counter and finding God already there.

CONTENTS

Part III: Beauty in the Basics

Part IV: Standing Tall (on the Counter)

Part V: Reaching Further

INTRODUCTION

You may be wondering why a guy would write a devotional for women, specifically moms.

I've been blessed by first having a mother who meant the world to me and taught me much about life. I draw all my faith, hope, and love from how she lived her life. I draw so much joy and optimism from every situation, thanks to how she helped mold my heart.

I've also been blessed to have a wife who is Mom to our three children. She's filled with faith, hope, and love and has a serving heart, an untiring connection with people, and a thirst for adventure. I've observed my wife for almost thirty years, and she has modeled prayers and petitions that I'd never dreamt of before. This book is devoted to them and to you.

This book is a fifty-two-week devotional for moms, but it's also my gift of devotion and gratitude to my mom and my wife. They deserve to know what an impact they have on the men and children in their lives. We may not always say it with the right words or actions—or even say it at all—but we all want the moms in our lives to know how much they are loved and cherished.

This book is for all moms at the various stages of parenting, whether you're a new mom, a step-mom, a mom of toddlers, tweens, or teens, or a mom of adult children. It's for stay-at-home moms and moms who have full-time or part-time jobs on top of your mom duties at home. Maybe you haven't heard or felt the gratitude for all the simple, everyday things you do and say to make your loved ones feel loved, welcomed, accepted, heard, and important.

Society and social media may make you feel like you fall short in some way, but this book is filled with prayers, scripture, words of encouragement, and gratitude, as well as a few inspirational songs to let you know how much you are loved and cherished and that you are enough.

For every article of clothing you've washed and folded, for every dishwasher you've filled and emptied, for every listening moment, and for every kind word, you are loved and treasured. May you find a gratitude that touches your heart and lets you know how much you mean to us dads and your children.

PART I

LIFE IS A LITTLE STICKY

THE SACRED SOUND OF THE DISHWASHER

Opening Reflection

Have you ever stood in your kitchen, surrounded by crumbs, dirty dishes, and the scent of reheated coffee—and unexpectedly felt at peace? The clink of dishes, the hum of the dishwasher, and even the light catching on a soap bubble can become the backdrop for something deeper: the realization that God's presence is woven into our routines, not just our mountaintop moments.

Scripture

> *"Whatever you do, work heartily, as for the Lord and not for men."*
> —Colossians 3:23 (ESV)

Devotional Thought

Somewhere along the way, we were told that purpose must be *big*—that making an impact means making headlines, and spiritual depth is found only in long prayers or mountain monasteries.

But what if holiness is hiding in your rinse cycle?

Today, we are invited to lean into the mundane—the counter wiping, sock folding, and email answering—not as distractions from our spiritual life, but as the very *center* of it. When we slow down and pay attention, we begin to see that our lives don't need to be sparkly to be sacred.

Jesus washed feet. He broke bread. He noticed fig trees. The divine often shows up in the ordinary, and so can we.

Prayer

Lord of dirty dishes and laundry piles,
Help me recognize You in the ordinary rhythms of my life.
Teach me to see my small tasks not as burdens,
But as beautiful, daily offerings.
Let me find joy in the everyday,
Knowing You are with me at the counter
Just as much as on the mountaintop.
Amen.

Simple Prompt or Challenge

This week, choose one daily task that you normally rush through—washing dishes, making lunch, tidying a room—and treat it as an act of worship. As you do it, thank God for each small blessing involved. Pause. Breathe. Be present.

_____

_____

_____

_____

_____

Optional Reflection Songs

- *Every Moment Holy* – Christy Nockels
- *This Is the Day* – Phil Wickham
- *Simple Gospel* – United Pursuit
- *Little Things with Great Love* – Audrey Assad

COFFEE STAINS AND CRUMBS OF HOPE

Opening Reflection

Have you ever spilled coffee right after cleaning the counter and felt the ridiculous sting of defeat? Or found yourself staring at toast crumbs like they hold the secrets of the universe? Life happens in these tiny moments—frustrating, unspectacular, and yet oddly profound.

Sometimes it's not the "big things" that test our faith, but the accumulation of small messes that seem to mock our efforts. However, maybe those very messes are grace notes in our day.

Scripture

> *"My grace is sufficient for you, for my power is made perfect in weakness."*
> —2 Corinthians 12:9a (NIV)

Devotional Thought

The kitchen counter is more than just a surface. It's a holy altar of real life. It catches the toast crumbs, the unopened mail, the scattered crayons, and the weight of our weary elbows. It's where we drop our keys, our shoulders, and sometimes our hope.

The counter is a metaphor for groundedness, for the things that are within reach even when the stars feel impossibly far away. Spilled coffee doesn't mean you've failed. It means you're living. Grace doesn't wait for your life to look tidy; it shows up sticky, strong, and sufficient.

When your day starts sideways, when you feel like you're behind before your feet even hit the floor—pause. Take a deep breath. God is already present in that moment, not waiting for your circumstances to improve before showing up.

Prayer

Dear God,
Help me to see You in the cluttered corners and coffee rings.
Teach me to welcome the crumbs as reminders that I'm here, alive, and sustained.
Even in my imperfections, Your grace spills over like a fresh cup,
And I'm thankful—for messes, for mornings, for You.
Amen.

Simple Prompt or Challenge

Tomorrow morning, before scrolling your phone or checking the time, stand at your kitchen counter and offer a silent prayer of gratitude, even if there are crumbs—especially if there are crumbs.

_____

_____

_____

_____

_____

_____

Optional Reflection Songs

- *Morning by Morning (I Will Trust)* – Pat Barrett
- *Gracefully Broken* – Matt Redman
- *New Wine* – Hillsong Worship
- *Come As You Are* – Crowder

Week 3

YOGA PANTS AND UNREALISTIC EXPECTATIONS

Opening Reflection

Have you ever worn yoga pants for an entire day without doing a single yoga pose? You're not alone. Sometimes yoga pants are survival gear—the spiritual armor of the overwhelmed. You often wear them not because you're on a fitness journey but because you're dodging the reality that you're not "together" today.

You scroll through curated photos and filtered lives on social media, all while standing in a kitchen that looks like a Pinterest fail. Yet God sees the holy in all of it—and in us.

Scripture

"The Lord does not look at the things people look at. People look at the outward appearance, but the Lord looks at the heart."

—1 Samuel 16:7b (NIV)

Devotional Thought

Social media has a way of turning comparison into a spiritual crisis. When everyone else seems to be hosting brunch in color-coordinated outfits while you're Googling "how to get slime out of a couch," it's easy to feel like you're failing.

But the truth is, God isn't grading your life on the same curve that Instagram is. He's not looking at the piles of unfolded laundry or whether your living room throw-pillows are arranged in threes. He sees the kindness you offered when you were tired, the prayer you whispered while stirring spaghetti, and the courage it took just to show up today.

Let your yoga pants become a symbol of reality over performance, of grace over guilt, and of choosing authenticity over appearance.

You don't have to "have it all together" to be loved by God. He's already chosen you, right in the mess.

Prayer

God who sees beyond the filters,
Thank You for loving me as I am—not as I pretend to be.
When I feel like I'm falling short, remind me that I'm enough in You.
Help me release unrealistic expectations
And embrace the grace of being real.
Amen.

Simple Prompt or Challenge

Pick one unrealistic expectation you've placed on yourself this week. Write it down. Then, write a truer, kinder version underneath it. Read the second one aloud every morning this week.

_____

_____

_____

_____

_____

_____

Optional Reflection Songs

- *You Say* – Lauren Daigle
- *Known* – Tauren Wells
- *Truth Be Told* – Matthew West
- *Good Grace* – Hillsong UNITED

___

THE MYTH OF BALANCE (PART 1)

Opening Reflection

There's a Pinterest-perfect version of "balance" that whispers: if you just try hard enough, schedule better, drink more water, and use color-coded calendars, life will finally feel smooth. But reality often feels more like you're juggling eggs while riding a unicycle—on a slope.

Let's be honest: balance is overrated. Joy is possible, even when you're teetering.

Scripture

> *"The joy of the Lord is your strength."*
> —Nehemiah 8:10b (NIV)

Devotional Thought

Life is rarely balanced—and that's okay. Sometimes it's less about having every category in order (faith, family, work, self-care) and more about showing up, with jelly on your hands and an open heart.

We often think spiritual maturity means mastering life like a monk with a perfectly centered soul. But maybe it's more like learning to wobble well. Maybe joy isn't found in the absence of chaos, but in our ability to smile mid-spin and trust God to keep us upright.

The myth of balance says, "Get it all under control." But grace says, "I'm with you in the chaos." That's good news, especially when the school project is due, the coffee is cold, and your prayer life feels like a voicemail on repeat.

You don't have to be steady to be faithful. You just have to keep showing up.

Prayer

God of all seasons and schedules,
Thank You for meeting me in the wobble.
When I feel pulled in a hundred directions,
Remind me that Your joy is my strength—
Not my schedule, not my performance, not my perfection.
Help me laugh, breathe, and lean on You
When I feel like I'm losing my balance.
Amen.

Simple Prompt or Challenge

This week, pick one area of your life where you feel like you're "dropping the ball." Instead of fixing it, *bless it*. Write a short note or prayer: "This is not perfect, but God is present here." Tape it to your fridge, planner, or mirror as a reminder.

_____

_____

_____

_____

_____

_____

Optional Reflection Songs

- *I Will Carry You* – Ellie Holcomb
- *Joy* – Rend Collective
- *Hold It All Together* – Lauren Daigle
- *He's Always Been Faithful* – Sara Groves

THE MYTH OF BALANCE (PART 2)

Opening Reflection

When was the last time someone asked, "How are you?" and you said, "Busy"? We live in a world that glorifies hustle and hands us planners like holy grails, as if balance is the ultimate sign of success.

But what if balance isn't the goal at all? What if the better pursuit is *presence*—showing up with joy, even when the scales feel wildly uneven?

Scripture

> *"Come to me, all you who are weary and burdened, and I will give you rest."*
> —Matthew 11:28 (NIV)

Devotional Thought

Balance is often marketed as the key to happiness. But if you've ever tried to do "everything well," you know that something always gives—whether it's mealtime, prayer time, or your patience.

Life isn't about executing a flawless schedule. It's about being honest with our limits and leaning into a God who doesn't grade us on our multitasking skills. Sometimes your prayer happens in the carpool line. Sometimes dinner is cereal—again. That doesn't mean you're failing. It means you're human.

The goal isn't perfect balance. It's joyful dependence. It's trusting that God doesn't need you to juggle everything; He simply wants you to trust Him with *something*—your mess, your exhaustion, your tiny, whispered yes.

The grace of Jesus meets us in the imbalance. In fact, it might just be the very place where His strength becomes most visible.

Prayer

Jesus,
I bring You my imbalance—the overflowing to-do list, the dishes in the sink, the prayers I meant to pray.
Remind me that I don't need to hold it all together. You already are.

Teach me to delight in the joy of being present,
Not in the illusion of being perfect.
Amen.

Simple Prompt or Challenge

This week, make a "Not-To-Do" list. Choose two or three things to intentionally set aside to protect your peace and presence. Tape it somewhere visible as an act of grace.

_____

_____

_____

_____

_____

_____

Optional Reflection Songs

- *Breathe* – Jonny Diaz
- *Be Still My Soul (In You I Rest)* – Kari Jobe
- *Come to Me* – Bethel Music & Jenn Johnson
- *Sparrows* – Cory Asbury

WHAT THE MESS MIGHT BE SAYING

Opening Reflection

We usually try to silence the mess. Hide it before guests arrive. Tuck it into drawers. Apologize for it before anyone can judge. But what if instead of rushing past it, we paused and listened? What if the mess isn't something to conquer, but something that's trying to speak?

Behind every pile of papers or laundry basket is a life in motion. And often, underneath the clutter is a quiet whisper of God's grace.

Scripture

> *"Search me, God, and know my heart;*
> *test me and know my anxious thoughts."*
> —Psalm 139:23 (NIV)

Devotional Thought

What happens when you spot a dust bunny under the fridge? Could it be a metaphor for your prayer life—sporadic, awkward, and honest? The profound truth is that God doesn't avoid our mess; He enters into it.

What if the pile on your counter is reminding you that your soul is weary?
What if your cluttered space mirrors your crowded heart?
What if the unanswered texts or unfolded clothes are gentle invitations to slow down—not because you're failing, but because you're human?

God doesn't use messes to shame us. He uses them to invite us. He knows that sometimes our external disarray reflects our internal overwhelm. And rather than handing us a chore chart, He offers us rest, grace, and renewal.

When we stop hiding our mess from God, we begin to understand how deeply loved we are—exactly as we are, not once we've cleaned up.

Prayer

God who sees beneath the surface,
Teach me to stop apologizing for the mess and start asking what it might reveal.
Search my heart—know what's tangled, tired, and cluttered.
Thank You for loving me as I am,

And for calling me to presence, not perfection.
Amen.

Simple Prompt or Challenge

Choose one space in your home that feels messy or neglected. Instead of rushing to fix it, spend five minutes simply sitting near it. As you do, ask God: "What are You inviting me to notice here—in my space, in my spirit?"

_____

_____

_____

_____

_____

_____

Optional Reflection Songs

- *Clean* – Natalie Grant
- *Come As You Are* – Crowder
- *Beautiful Things* – Gungor
- *Holy Spirit* – Francesca Battistelli

THE GOSPEL OF THE GROCERY LIST

Opening Reflection

The grocery list is rarely seen as sacred. It's a scribbled mess of bananas, paper towels, lunch meat, and that one thing you'll forget unless it's underlined three times.

But maybe that list—the one shoved in your purse or typed in your Notes app—is more spiritual than you realize. Maybe it's a sign of love, provision, and a God who shows up in the cereal aisle.

Scripture

> *"So whether you eat or drink or whatever you do, do it all for the glory of God."*
> —1 Corinthians 10:31 (NIV)

Devotional Thought

Let us celebrate ordinary tasks—not in spite of their simplicity but because of it. And what's more ordinary than a grocery run?

Think about what's on your list: food to nourish, snacks to soothe, supplies to sustain your people. You plan, prepare, and provide—not for applause but because love moves quietly like that.

Jesus multiplied loaves and fish. He fed the hungry with what seemed like not enough. He turned water into wine at a wedding feast. Our grocery lists may not seem miraculous, but the love they represent—the unseen labor, the quiet anticipation of needs—is Kingdom work.

There is a gospel in the way we shop, cook, and care—not a flashy one, a faithful one.

So the next time you're standing in line with your cart full of life's needs, remember that God meets you in Aisle 4 just as much as in the pew.

Prayer

God of milk and honey—and almond butter,
Thank You for being present in my planning,
In my daily decisions, and in the details I overlook.
Remind me that small acts of care carry great significance.

Let me see my errands as expressions of love
And even my grocery list as a kind of prayer.
Amen.

Simple Prompt or Challenge

Take your grocery list (or create one this week), and next to each item, jot down one word of gratitude for the person you're buying it for. Let your list become a litany of thankfulness.

_____

_____

_____

_____

_____

_____

Optional Reflection Songs

- *Give Me Jesus* – Fernando Ortega
- *The Heart of Worship* – Matt Redman
- *Daily Bread* – United Pursuit
- *God of the Ordinary* – Jon Guerra
- *Milk & Honey* – David Crowder

YOU'RE NOT BEHIND— YOU'RE HUMAN

Opening Reflection

There's a constant ticking in the background of our lives—a voice that says, "You're behind." Behind on emails, laundry, spiritual growth, self-care, meal planning, parenting, and even breathing.

But what if "behind" isn't the truth? What if it's just a lie whispered by comparison and perfectionism—and the truth is this: You're right on time because you are human, not a machine.

Scripture

> *"He remembers that we are dust."*
> —Psalm 103:14b (ESV)

Devotional Thought

We were never created to keep pace with the internet or match the energy of our productivity culture. God never asked us to finish every task or meet every expectation. He asked us to walk with Him—*walk*, not sprint.

Release the illusion of having it all together. That includes letting go of the idea that you're somehow spiritually or emotionally behind. That feeling comes from the world's standards—not God's.

God knows your bandwidth. He knows your limits. He knows that some days you'll barely get through your to-do list, and others, you'll feel a sacred victory in remembering to drink water.

You're not behind; you're being held. And that's more than enough.

Prayer

Lord of grace and gentle truth,
Quiet the voice that tells me I should be further along.
Remind me that I am not a disappointment;
I am deeply known and deeply loved.
Help me trade hustle for healing,
And live my days with mercy, not measurement.
Amen.

Simple Prompt or Challenge

This week, whenever you catch yourself thinking, *I should be further along,* pause and replace it with, *I'm doing the best I can. That is holy.* Write this somewhere visible: "God is not in a hurry with me."

_____

_____

_____

_____

_____

_____

Optional Reflection Songs

- *Come Rest* – Lindsey Maestas
- *You're Gonna Be OK* – Jenn Johnson
- *Mercy Is a Song* – Matthew West
- *I Am Not Alone* – Kari Jobe

BURNT TOAST THEOLOGY

Opening Reflection

You had the best intentions: a wholesome breakfast, a peaceful morning, a productive start. Then—the smell, not of fresh-baked goodness but of scorched toast and something that might set off the smoke alarm.

Life has a way of turning even simple plans crispy. However, maybe burnt toast can still preach.

Scripture

> *"My flesh and my heart may fail, but God is the strength of my heart and my portion forever."*
> —Psalm 73:26 (NIV)

Devotional Thought

There's something oddly humbling about burning the toast. It's a reminder that even our most basic tasks can go sideways—that despite our best efforts, messes happen. And when they do, we usually react with frustration or self-judgment.

But maybe the burnt toast is a metaphor for life's unpredictability and the grace available in it. The toast is too dark, the coffee's cold, someone's crying (possibly you), and the day hasn't even started. Still, there's God—amid the fumes—saying, "I'm with you—even here."

We often believe that spiritual maturity looks like unflustered calm. But what if it actually looks like laughing when things go wrong? Or choosing to sit down anyway, with a plate of second-best breakfast, and say, "Thank You, Lord."

Burnt toast theology says: I didn't get it all right today, but I showed up. And God did, too.

Prayer

God of golden brown and blackened edges,
Thank You for showing up in burnt breakfasts and broken routines.
When I fall short—again—remind me that You're not disappointed.
You're delighted to sit with me, even in the mess.
Let grace rise in my heart, even when the toast doesn't.
Amen.

Simple Prompt or Challenge

Next time something goes wrong this week—burned food, missed appointment, forgotten detail—pause and say, "This is not a failure. This is life. And God is still here." Bonus: share it with someone and let it become laughter.

_____

_____

_____

_____

_____

_____

Optional Reflection Songs

- *God of the Mundane* – Nathan Peterson
- *Grace Wins* – Matthew West
- *Joy Comes in the Morning* – Baylor Wilson
- *This Is the Stuff* – Francesca Battistelli

PEACE IN THE PILE OF SOCKS

Opening Reflection

There's something particularly humbling about sorting socks. They rarely match, some are mysteriously missing, and none spark joy. Yet there's a quiet rhythm to it, a whisper of order in the everyday shuffle.

What if peace doesn't wait for the big moments? What if it waits for us in the sock basket?

Scripture

"You will keep in perfect peace those whose minds are steadfast, because they trust in you."
—Isaiah 26:3 (NIV)

Devotional Thought

Holiness often hides in humble tasks. The pile of socks, the crumbs on the counter, the never-ending cycle of dishes—these are not the obstacles to our spiritual life. They *are* the spiritual life.

Sorting socks is a kind of prayer. It's an act of care done quietly, thanklessly, repeatedly—like faith, like love.

There is peace to be found in the repetition of simple things, not because they're exciting but because they root us in presence. They remind us of who we care for, who we are becoming, and the God who finds beauty in our smallest offerings.

Peace doesn't require silence or solitude. Sometimes it simply requires us to slow down enough to notice what's right in front of us—like two matching socks.

Prayer

God of quiet moments and scattered socks,
Thank You for meeting me in the middle of my daily rhythms.
When life feels tangled or incomplete,
Anchor me in the present moment with You.
Help me find peace, not in perfection,
But in Your steady, loving presence.
Amen.

Simple Prompt or Challenge

The next time you're doing a repetitive task (laundry, dishes, wiping the table), turn it into a breath prayer. Inhale, "You are here." Exhale, "I am at peace." Let the moment become a sanctuary.

_____

_____

_____

_____

_____

_____

Optional Reflection Songs

- *It Is Well (Through It All)* – Kristene DiMarco
- *Peace Be Still* – Hope Darst
- *Simple Things* – Sandra McCracken
- *Still* – Amanda Lindsey Cook

GOD IS NOT AFRAID OF MESSES

Opening Reflection

We clean up before company comes over. We hide the unfolded laundry, stuff junk drawers, and light a candle to mask the scent of fish from two nights ago.

We do the same with God sometimes—presenting only the polished parts, the Sunday versions of ourselves. However, God isn't impressed by tidiness. He's not after your performance. He's after your presence—even in the mess.

Scripture

> *"But God demonstrates his own love for us in this: While we were still sinners, Christ died for us."*
> —Romans 5:8 (NIV)

Devotional Thought

Have you ever vacuumed before Bible study and felt smug about it—as though clean floors equal spiritual readiness?

We've all been there. The temptation to measure holiness by appearances is real.

But the truth is that God does some of His best work in our mess—not just the laundry piles and sticky counters but the doubts, the sadness, the forgotten prayers. He doesn't walk away from our clutter. He sits with us in it.

God's love isn't reserved for the version of you that has it all together. He loves the real you right now—the one running behind, emotionally tired, spiritually hungry, and still doing your best.

You don't have to wait until the mess is cleaned up to invite Him in. He's already there with grace in His hands and zero judgment in His heart.

Prayer

Jesus,
Thank You for stepping into my mess without hesitation.
You never flinch at my weakness or turn away from my clutter.
Help me stop pretending,
And instead come to You honestly
Because I know You'll meet me with kindness, not condemnation.
Amen.

WEEK 11: GOD IS NOT AFRAID OF MESSES

Simple Prompt or Challenge

This week, spend five quiet minutes in a messy space—your house, your car, your heart. Resist the urge to clean or fix. Simply invite God to be with you in it. Breathe and say, "You are welcome here, Lord—even now."

_____

_____

_____

_____

_____

_____

Optional Reflection Songs

- *Come As You Are* – Crowder
- *You Love Me Anyway* – Sidewalk Prophets
- *Grace That Is Greater* – Austin Stone Worship
- *Nothing to Prove* – Phillips, Craig & Dean

HOLY INTERRUPTIONS (AND COLD COFFEE)

Opening Reflection

You warm the coffee, set it down, forget about it, warm it again, and sit down. Someone yells; something spills. Repeat. By the time you finally take a sip, your coffee is room temperature, and your nerves are slightly frayed.

Interruptions can feel like obstacles to the real day. However, maybe the interruptions *are* the real day, and God is in the middle of them.

Scripture

> *"The heart of man plans his way,*
> *but the Lord establishes his steps."*
> —Proverbs 16:9 (ESV)

Devotional Thought

Cold coffee is more than a parenting cliché or a mark of a chaotic morning. It's a symbol of how our plans constantly bump up against reality.

You meant to sit with your Bible, but someone needed cereal. You were going to journal, but your inbox exploded. You planned for quiet, and life handed you loud—again.

God doesn't need a cleared schedule to show up. He often arrives in the unplanned, between the spilled milk and the text you didn't expect. Holy interruptions aren't mistakes. They're invitations to see God in real time.

What if your day wasn't derailed? What if it was just re-routed by grace?

Maybe the best spiritual moments aren't the perfectly lit, Instagram-able ones. Maybe they're when you pause with lukewarm coffee and realize: *God is with me here, too.*

Prayer

God of cold coffee and constant interruptions,
Help me to stop waiting for "perfect" moments to meet with You.
Let me see Your presence in the chaos and the unexpected.
Teach me to welcome interruptions as reminders
That You are always near,

Especially when I feel off track.
Amen.

Simple Prompt or Challenge

Pick one moment this week when your plans are interrupted.
Instead of rushing to fix it or push through, pause. Whisper,
"God, what are You showing me here?" Let the interruption
become an invitation.

_____

_____

_____

_____

_____

_____

Optional Reflection Songs

- *Interruptions* – Amanda Cook (live version
  recommended)
- *You're With Me* – Highlands Worship
- *This Is the Day* – Phil Wickham
- *Look What You've Done* – Tasha Layton

PART II

ORDINARY LOVE

THE SACRED WORK OF MISMATCHED SOCKS

Opening Reflection

If love languages included "tolerating sock chaos," some of us would be fluent. One person folds socks into perfect pairs; the other grabs two clean ones and calls it a win.

Marriage—and any long-term partnership—isn't made in candlelight moments. It's made in repeated acts of quiet care, like noticing the sock drawer is empty and doing something about it.

Scripture

> *"Be completely humble and gentle;*
> *be patient, bearing with one another in love."*
> —Ephesians 4:2 (NIV)

Devotional Thought

God's kind of love lives not in grand romantic gestures, but in the humble rhythm of ordinary life—like folding socks, locking the door, and making the coffee because your spouse got to bed late last night.

This isn't the kind of love that trends on social media. It's deeper. It doesn't sparkle; it sustains.

Marriage and love are not measured in perfect harmony but in the sacred practice of "bearing with." That doesn't mean tolerating one another in misery; it means leaning in, day after day, when you're both tired, both flawed, and still choosing to care.

The beauty of mismatched socks is that they still get the job done—just like us: imperfect, frayed at the edges, but held together by grace.

Prayer

God of faithful love,
Thank You for the ordinary ways love shows up,
For small acts of service, quiet forgiveness, and shared socks.
Teach me to love not for applause but for presence.
Help me see the sacred in these unseen moments
Where real love lives and lasts.
Amen.

Simple Prompt or Challenge

Choose one small, intentional act of love to do for your spouse, partner, or close friend this week, something quiet but kind: a text, a chore, a cup of coffee, a moment of listening. Don't announce it—just offer it. Let it be a sock-folding kind of love.

_____

_____

_____

_____

_____

_____

Optional Reflection Songs

- *When I Say I Do* – Matthew West
- *Love Never Fails* – Brandon Heath
- *Holding Hands* – Steve Green
- *Divine Romance* – Phil Wickham
- *Country Psalm* – Brandon Lake

LOVE IN THE LITTLE THINGS

Opening Reflection

It's not usually the big, cinematic moments that define a relationship. It's the way she remembers how you take your coffee. The fact that he fills up your gas tank without saying a word. It's the familiar "Did you lock the door?" or the soft sigh of shared silence at the end of a long day.

Love doesn't always arrive with fireworks. Sometimes it hums like a fridge and smells like reheated leftovers.

Scripture

> *"Let all that you do be done in love."*
> —1 Corinthians 16:14 (ESV)

Devotional Thought

Little things are the heart of enduring love—not the stuff of fairy tales, but the rituals of real life: dishes, creamers, closing laptop lids, late-night check-ins, and yes—remembering to buy the good toilet paper.

It's tempting to think that love has to be profound or poetic to count. However, some of the most powerful expressions of love are so ordinary that they're nearly invisible. And yet, they keep people tethered, seen, and safe.

God's love often shows up in the small things, too—a sunrise, a stranger's kindness, a whisper in the chaos: "I'm still here." He modeled a kind of love that washed feet, broke bread, and blessed ordinary moments. When we love like that, we reflect Him more clearly than we realize.

The little things are not little at all.

Prayer

Lord of small gestures and deep love,
Thank You for daily chances to love well.
Help me notice, serve, and show up
In ways that feel small but mean the world.
Let me become fluent in this quiet language of kindness
That speaks louder than words.
Amen.

Simple Prompt or Challenge

Make a list of five little things someone does that make you feel loved. Then flip it—write down five things you can intentionally do this week to show love through small, unnoticed acts.

_____

_____

_____

_____

_____

_____

Optional Reflection Songs

- *Love Will Hold Us Together* – Matt Maher
- *The Little Things* – JJ Heller
- *Make Room* – Community Music
- *This Is Love* – For King & Country

THE ART OF STAYING PRESENT

Opening Reflection

You're in the middle of tying a shoe, checking a text, and stirring the spaghetti—all at once. A voice calls from another room. A meltdown begins. You can't remember when you last sat still without something buzzing, boiling, or breaking.

Yet, in the middle of this beautiful mess, someone just wants to know: *Are you here—really here?*

Scripture

> *"Be still, and know that I am God."*
> —Psalm 46:10a
> (NIV)

Devotional Thought

Presence is the rarest of gifts in a distracted world. Parenting and family life are not something you master, but something you show up for—again and again. Tantrums, eye rolls, bed-time stalls, teenage silences—all of it.

Staying present doesn't mean you have perfect answers or boundless patience. It means you stop long enough to notice the way their eyes look when they're telling you a story, the small moments that flicker and disappear if you're not watching.

God is never distracted. He never forgets to listen. And He invites us into that kind of attentiveness, not just for our families but for ourselves. Staying present is an act of love, an act of worship, and a brave, quiet way to say, "You matter more than my to-do list."

You won't do it perfectly. That's not the point. The goal isn't control; it's connection.

Prayer

God of now,
Teach me the discipline of presence.
Help me look up, lean in, and slow down.
Let me offer my full attention to the ones I love—
Not just when it's easy but when it's loud and complicated.
Make me present like You are present: steady, patient,
and kind.
Amen.

Simple Prompt or Challenge

Put your phone down for one hour a day this week and intentionally spend that hour being fully present with someone:
reading aloud, listening, walking, or just being still together.
Watch what changes in you.

_____

_____

_____

_____

_____

_____

Optional Reflection Songs

- *Be Still* – The Fray (acoustic)
- *The Gift of Presence* – Salt of Sound
- *Slow Down* – Nichole Nordeman
- *Come Close* – Jenn Johnson
- *Hard Fought Hallelujah* – Brandon Lake/Jelly Roll

LETTING GO OF PERFECT

Opening Reflection

The craft wasn't Pinterest-worthy. The lasagna was store-bought. You lost your temper, forgot picture day, and said, "Just five more minutes" too many times.

You wanted to be the mom, the friend, the spouse who nails it. But today, you're just surviving, and it feels like it's not enough.

However, what if not being perfect is exactly where grace begins?

Scripture

> *"He gives strength to the weary and*
> *increases the power of the weak."*
> —Isaiah 40:29 (NIV)

Devotional Thought

We must dismantle the illusion of perfect parenting and polished womanhood. The idea that a meaningful life must be mess-free, well-scheduled, and well-documented is a heavy burden to carry—and an unnecessary one.

Your children don't need a flawless mom. Your spouse doesn't need a curated partner. Your friends don't need an always-cheerful version of you. They need someone present and honest—someone willing to say, "I'm sorry" and "I'm trying."

And what's more, *God* doesn't require perfection from you, either. In fact, your weakness isn't an obstacle to Him. It's the very space where His grace flows in.

The pressure to do it all, look the part, and never fall apart is a lie. Letting go of perfect isn't giving up. It's waking up to what really matters.

Prayer

Lord,
I confess my need to be enough for everyone—
And I confess it's wearing me out.
Thank You for meeting me in the middle of my mess,
For not needing me to perform,
Just to come honestly.
Help me love others—not perfectly,
But fully, and in Your strength.
Amen.

Simple Prompt or Challenge

Name one thing you're trying to perfect this week, whether it's a birthday party, a parenting moment, or your image. Write it down. Then write across it: "Grace is better than perfect." Practice repeating this each time your inner critic shows up.

_____

_____

_____

_____

_____

_____

Optional Reflection Songs

- *Broken Vessels (Amazing Grace)* – Hillsong Worship
- *You Don't Miss a Thing* – Amanda Cook
- *Gracefully Broken* – Matt Redman
- *He Knows My Name* – Francesca Battistelli

Week 17

TANTRUMS, TEENS, AND TENDER MERCIES

Opening Reflection

There's a unique moment—somewhere between stepping on a LEGO and arguing with a teenager about curfews—when you question everything: your parenting strategies, your patience, your calling, and your sanity.

However, in that storm of noise, sass, spills, and slammed doors, something else is present, too: mercy—quiet, stubborn, faithful mercy.

Scripture

> *"Because of the Lord's great love, we are not consumed, for his compassions never fail. They are new every morning; great is your faithfulness."*
>
> —Lamentations 3:22–23 (NIV)

Devotional Thought

Being a parent isn't about control; it's about presence—laughing through tantrums, sitting through silence, and holding steady when the script you imagined for your family is nowhere in sight.

Children have a way of bringing out both our best and our most frayed selves. They uncover our limits and invite us into a deeper understanding of God's mercy. Because parenting, more than almost anything else, teaches us to rely on grace, not just extend it.

Tantrums may test your patience. Teens may test your wisdom. But both offer moments to practice unconditional love—not because we're saints but because we're growing alongside our children.

You're not failing because it's hard. You're not weak because you feel overwhelmed. You're human. And God's mercies are new every morning—yes, even the ones that start with screaming.

Prayer

Lord of mercy and motherhood,
Thank You for meeting me in the chaos—
In the tears, the backtalk, the mess, and the beauty.
When I lose my patience, remind me of Your unending kindness.

Teach me to parent not from perfection, but from grace.
And when I've reached my limit,
Let Your mercy begin again in me.
Amen.

Simple Prompt or Challenge

Choose a tough parenting moment from this past week.
Instead of replaying what you could have done better, name
one merciful thing you did: a deep breath, a kind word, not
slamming the door. Write it down and say, "That was grace
in motion."

_____

_____

_____

_____

_____

_____

Optional Reflection Songs

- *Mercy* – Matt Redman
- *Lord, I Need You* – Matt Maher
- *New Every Morning* – Audrey Assad
- *Goodness of God* – CeCe Winans

Week 18

TARGET AISLES AND SACRED FRIENDSHIPS

Opening Reflection

There's something oddly spiritual about pushing a red cart through Target with a friend, sharing both silence and over-shares between the dollar section and the seasonal mugs. You didn't plan to bare your soul in the cleaning aisle—but there you are, tearing up next to Clorox wipes.

These are the holy moments—not scheduled but sacred, nonetheless.

Scripture

"A friend loves at all times, and a brother is born for adversity."
—Proverbs 17:17 (NIV)

Devotional Thought

Friendship is celebrated not in perfectly hosted brunches but in the mundane rituals of life: running errands, texting memes, knowing each other's favorite snacks. Deep friendships often don't form over planned connection events. They form in shared carts and cracked heels. They're built on realness.

You need friends who will tell you you're not crazy, even when you've worn the same yoga pants three days in a row, friends who know the names of your kids' teachers and who send you a GIF instead of a long text because they just know.

These friendships are not extra. They are essential. They remind us that we are not alone—not in parenting, not in grief, not in hormone-ridden days or hope-starved seasons.

Jesus had friends. He wept with them, walked with them, and fed them. We were never meant to carry life alone, especially not the parts that make us feel tired, unseen, or too much.

So yes, Target can be holy ground. So can your porch, your minivan, your texts, and anywhere love shows up with truth and snacks.

Prayer

God of unexpected sacred spaces,
Thank You for friends who see past my words
And love me in my Target runs and tired days.

Help me be that kind of friend—
Present, honest, and quick to show up with laughter or grace.
Bless the friendships that hold us together
When life feels too big to handle alone.
Amen.

Simple Prompt or Challenge

Text one friend today who knows your fridge or who has seen your mess and stayed. Say three words: "Thank you, friend." Then, tell them one specific thing you value about their presence in your life.

_____

_____

_____

_____

_____

_____

Optional Reflection Songs

- *Lean on Me* – Bill Withers
- *With You* – Elevation Rhythm
- *Find You Here* – Ellie Holcomb
- *Your Love Defends Me* – Matt Maher

Week 19

THE PEOPLE WHO KNOW YOUR FRIDGE

Opening Reflection

There are friends who knock politely. And then there are friends who walk in without asking, help themselves to something from your fridge, and hand you a Diet Coke while you're still in your pajamas.

These are the friends who've seen your fridge at its worst and stayed, the ones who see your unfiltered life and still love you, not in spite of it but because of it.

Scripture

> *"Carry each other's burdens, and in this way,*
> *you will fulfill the law of Christ."*
> —Galatians 6:2 (NIV)

Devotional Thought

Let's celebrate friendships that are formed in real places—crumb-filled kitchens, unmade beds, open fridges. These aren't the friendships built on curated social media posts or polite dinner parties. These are the people who show up when your house is a wreck, your face is puffy, and your soul is heavy.

They are the people who *carry your burdens*—and sometimes your toddlers, your casseroles, or your emotional baggage. They know your fridge is mostly condiments and string cheese, and they don't judge.

This kind of friendship is rare. However, when it happens, it reflects the very heart of Christ, who never waited for people to clean up before sitting down with them.

We all need people who love us in our real lives. And you are called to be that kind of person, too. The kind who enters without needing an invitation. The kind who says, "What's in your fridge doesn't scare me. I'm here for the long haul."

Prayer

Jesus,
Thank You for the friends who have seen my mess and didn't flinch.
Help me treasure these rare, real connections—
To show up honestly and love generously.

Make me someone who carries burdens
And who never turns away from someone else's fridge full
of leftovers and life.
Amen.

Simple Prompt or Challenge

Invite a friend over without cleaning up first. Let your unfiltered life be seen. Or send a text that starts with, "Just so you know, this is what's really going on with me." Let someone see your "fridge" this week—and be that kind of friend in return.

_____

_____

_____

_____

_____

_____

Optional Reflection Songs

- *Brother* – NEEDTOBREATHE ft. Gavin DeGraw
- *Real Thing* – Dante Bowe
- *Be Kind* – Zak Abel & Sinead Harnett
- *As I Am* – Hillsong Young & Free

TEXTS, TEARS, AND HOLY CONNECTION

Opening Reflection

It starts with a simple "Thinking of you," or maybe a teary emoji. Maybe it's a shared meme that says, "I get it," or a voice memo at 10:42 p.m. because the day was just too much.

These aren't just digital exchanges. These are sacred echoes of presence—the kind of presence that says, "You are not alone."

Scripture

"Rejoice with those who rejoice; mourn with those who mourn."
   —Romans 12:15 (NIV)

Devotional Thought

What's more ordinary than the buzz of a phone?

But that buzz can become a blessing. A simple text can be a lifeline. A voice memo can be a prayer. A GIF can be grace in disguise. These moments may seem small, but they tether us to each other—and to God.

When you send a kind word to someone in tears or when someone sends one to you, something holy happens. You're not just replying; you're bearing witness. You're reminding someone that their emotions matter, that their moment matters, and that they matter.

Jesus didn't just preach to crowds. He wept with friends. He looked people in the eyes. He touched, listened, and lingered. He offered presence before answers.

We can do that, too. Even through a screen. Especially through compassion.

Prayer

Jesus,
Thank You for the friends who show up with soft words
and shared tears.
Teach me to be someone who listens well,
Who sends light into someone else's dark room,
And who isn't afraid to feel deeply or stay present.
Let my messages be mini-sermons of love—
Not perfect, just real.
Amen.

Simple Prompt or Challenge

Scroll through your messages. Pick one person you haven't checked on in a while. Send a short text: "You came to mind today. How are you really?" Offer a moment of presence through the ordinary. Let it become sacred.

_____

_____

_____

_____

_____

_____

Optional Reflection Songs

- *You Will Be Found* – Natalie Grant & Cory Asbury
- *Let It Matter* – Ellie Holcomb
- *Closer Than You Know* – Hillsong UNITED
- *I'm With You* – Nichole Nordeman

FRIENDSHIP WITHOUT FILTERS

Opening Reflection

We live in a world of filters: camera filters, life filters, even emotional ones. Smile emojis over sadness. "I'm fine" over "I'm falling apart." But the best friendships aren't curated. They're real.

They're the ones where you can take off the mask and breathe—ugly cry and all.

Scripture

> *"Therefore, encourage one another and build each other up, just as in fact you are doing."*
> —1 Thessalonians 5:11 (NIV)

Devotional Thought

The most meaningful relationships don't happen in polished living rooms or perfect conversations. They happen in sweatpants and over reheated leftovers while kids interrupt and the dishwasher hums in the background.

Friendship without filters means being the kind of person who can say, "This is me today—messy, moody, and still showing up." And having someone reply, "I'm so glad you did."

There's nothing quite like being fully seen and still fully loved. It's healing. It's rare. It's what Jesus offers—and what we can offer to one another.

The world doesn't need more perfectly curated friendships. It needs more honest ones, built not on comparison but compassion, not on performance but presence.

Take off the filter. Let someone see the real you. That's where connection begins.

Prayer

God of truth and tenderness,
Thank You for the friends who love the unedited me.
Teach me to show up for others with the same grace—
To be a soft place for honesty,
A steady hand for the shaky days,
And a reminder that they don't have to be perfect to be deeply loved.
Amen.

Simple Prompt or Challenge

Invite a friend into your unfiltered life this week. Send a message that doesn't have a neat bow, just honesty. Or invite someone over without cleaning up. Practice letting someone see your real and love you in it.

_____

_____

_____

_____

_____

_____

Optional Reflection Songs

- *You Love Me Anyway* – Sidewalk Prophets
- *Real Love* – Blanca
- *Known* – Tauren Wells
- *Come Out of Hiding* – Steffany Gretzinger

LOVE IS PATIENT (EVEN WHEN YOU'RE NOT)

Opening Reflection

Patience sounds poetic when read at weddings. It looks different, though, in the school pickup line, during toddler meltdowns, or when a loved one is taking forever to change their mind—or their socks.

Real love is rarely romantic in those moments. But that's when it becomes most real.

Scripture

> *"Love is patient, love is kind. It does not envy,*
> *it does not boast, it is not proud."*
>
> —1 Corinthians 13:4 (NIV)

Devotional Thought

"Love is patient." We've heard it a thousand times. But *living it*—that's the spiritual workout.

The ordinary spaces of life become classrooms for learning this kind of love. The interruptions. The repeated conversations. The way someone loads the dishwasher the wrong way again. These are not just frustrations to endure; they're invitations to grow.

Patience isn't pretending not to be annoyed. It's choosing presence over reaction. It's deciding to pause instead of push, to *stay* when you'd rather storm out, and to respond with grace when your nerves are frayed.

And the truth is, you won't always get it right. That's okay. Love isn't a test; it's a practice—a lifelong one. But the more we return to Jesus—the One who never rushes our growth—the more we'll find the patience to offer others the same space to be in progress.

Prayer

Jesus,
You've been endlessly patient with me—
With my wandering, my delays, my stubborn heart.
Help me offer that same gentle grace
To the people around me,
Especially when I feel impatient or stretched thin.

Teach me to love not just in words,
But in slowness, silence, and steadiness.
Amen.

Simple Prompt or Challenge

Identify one relationship or situation this week where you often feel impatient. Before reacting, take a breath and pray, "Lord, help me love here." Write it down. Place it somewhere visible. Let patience become your practice.

_____

_____

_____

_____

_____

_____

Optional Reflection Songs

- *Slow Down* – Nichole Nordeman
- *Love Never Fails* – Brandon Heath
- *Patience Love* – Cory Alstad
- *He's Always Been Faithful* – Sara Groves

Week 23

THE MINISTRY OF SHOWING UP

Opening Reflection

You didn't bring a casserole. You didn't have the perfect words. You weren't sure what to do.

But you showed up. You sat on the couch. You held their hand. You answered the text. And somehow, that was everything.

Scripture

> *"If one part suffers, every part suffers with it; if one part is honored, every part rejoices with it."*
> —Corinthians 12:26 (NIV)

Devotional Thought

There's a quiet kind of love that doesn't make headlines. It doesn't post selfies or gather applause. It's the kind of love that drives across town just to sit, answers phone calls at awkward hours, drops off a favorite snack, listens to silence, and doesn't try to fix what can't be fixed.

Faith isn't always loud. Sometimes it's low and steady. That's what showing up is—a kind of ministry that whispers, "You're not alone."

You don't need grand gestures. You need presence because presence is power. God doesn't always call us to solve someone's pain. Often, He simply calls us to share it.

Jesus was the embodiment of this kind of love. He came close. He wept. He lingered. He stayed. When we do the same, we reflect His heart more than we ever could with perfect words.

Prayer

Lord,
Teach me the quiet ministry of presence.
Let me be the kind of person who answers the hard texts,
Sits in hard places,
And trusts that my presence—flawed and unsure—is enough.
Make me less about fixing,
And more about faithfully showing up.
Amen.

Simple Prompt or Challenge

Think of someone in your life who is walking through a hard or lonely season. Don't overthink it—just reach out. Send a text. Drop by. Sit. Stay. Let your presence do the work.

_____

_____

_____

_____

_____

_____

Optional Reflection Songs

- *Let It Matter* – Ellie Holcomb
- *You Will Be Found* – Natalie Grant & Cory Asbury
- *Come What May* – We Are Messengers
- *If You Want Me To* – Ginny Owens

LOVING PEOPLE IN YOGA PANTS

Opening Reflection

Some days, love looks like putting on real pants and showing up with a casserole. However, more often, love looks like showing up in yoga pants—with dry shampoo in your hair, a wrinkled T-shirt, and just enough energy to say, "I'm here."

It turns out that's more than enough.

Scripture

> *"Above all, love each other deeply,*
> *because love covers over a multitude of sins."*
> —1 Peter 4:8 (NIV)

Devotional Thought

Sometimes yoga pants become more than comfy clothes; they become a symbol of real life. They're the uniform of the honest woman, the weary mom, the faithful friend who isn't trying to impress anyone—just trying to be there.

Loving people in yoga pants means loving them without the need to perform. It means inviting people into your cluttered home or into your tired day and offering what you have: yourself—even when you feel like it's not polished or enough.

The beauty is this: God doesn't need your outer life to be ironed out before He uses you. In fact, He often works best through the unpolished moments. Through the text you send, even though you're drained. Through the quick prayer you whisper when someone comes to mind. Through the casserole you bought, not made.

Love in yoga pants is real. It's resilient. It's the kind of love that lasts.

Prayer

God of real life and stretch waistbands,
Thank You for reminding me that I don't have to be impressive—
Just present.
Help me love others from where I am,
Even when I feel tired, messy, or unworthy.
Remind me that what I offer in grace and honesty
Matters more than perfection.
Amen.

Simple Prompt or Challenge

Invite someone into your day without putting on a mask—emotional or literal. Call, text, or meet them just as you are. Let yourself be seen. And let your kindness flow from comfort, not performance.

_____

_____

_____

_____

_____

_____

Optional Reflection Songs

- *Come As You Are* – Crowder
- *Real Love* – Blanca
- *Flawless* – MercyMe
- *You Already Know* – JJ Heller

PART III
BEAUTY IN THE BASICS

DUST BUNNIES AND DEVOTIONALS

Opening Reflection

You meant to have a quiet devotional this morning. Instead, you chased a dust bunny that you're pretty sure is older than your youngest child under the fridge with a broom. You sighed, tugged at your yoga pants, and thought, *This probably doesn't count as holy.*

But what if it does?

Scripture

> *"Serve wholeheartedly, as if you were serving the Lord, not people."*
> —Ephesians 6:7 (NIV)

Devotional Thought

Sometimes the spiritual life looks less like a mountaintop and more like sweatpants and sweeping.

Housekeeping and faith have more in common than we realize. Both require repetition. Both involve uncovering things we'd rather ignore. Both invite us to show up consistently, even when no one notices.

That dust bunny under the fridge is not just dirt. It's a reminder that messes accumulate when we're not looking—just like worry, bitterness, or apathy. And like our homes, our hearts need regular attention—not perfection, just presence.

God is not limited to quiet rooms and open Bibles. He meets us while we wipe the counter, fold the socks, and scrub the bathroom sink and toilet. These are not distractions from the sacred. They are sacred because He's there.

Prayer

God who dwells in every corner,
Thank You for being present in my daily tasks.
Help me see my routines not as interruptions,
But as invitations to connect with You.
Let even my cleaning become a kind of prayer,
And my house, a holy place where grace is sweeping through.
Amen.

Simple Prompt or Challenge

As you clean something this week—no matter how small—pray as you go. Use the time to talk to God about what's collecting in your heart. As you wipe or sweep, ask Him to refresh you from the inside out.

_____

_____

_____

_____

_____

_____

Optional Reflection Songs

- *Simple Gospel* – United Pursuit
- *Make Room* – Community Music
- *Sanctuary* – CeCe Winans
- *Every Moment Holy* – Christy Nockels

WHEN GOD MEETS YOU AT THE FRIDGE

Opening Reflection

It's not glamorous, and you've done it a hundred times: open the fridge, stare at the contents, forget what you came for, close it, then open it again two minutes later as if something new will magically appear.

You're not alone. And surprisingly, you're not far from holy ground either.

Scripture

> *"Surely the Lord is in this place, and I was not aware of it."*
> —Genesis 28:16 (NIV)

Devotional Thought

The kitchen—the fridge, the counter, the clutter—isn't just a setting. It's a sanctuary, a place where God doesn't wait for us to sit quietly with our coffee and a highlighter. He meets us where we already are.

The fridge moment—the pause, the search, the sigh—can feel like a metaphor for our spiritual hunger. Sometimes we don't even know what we're looking for. We just know something feels empty.

And into that space steps God—not with a lecture or a lightning bolt but with quiet presence: "I see you—even here."

Jacob had his moment of awe in the wilderness with a rock for a pillow. You might have yours in front of the veggie drawer. Either way, it counts.

God meets us in the real and routine. We don't have to be emotionally ready or spiritually impressive. We only have to be open—even if that means standing barefoot, distracted, and hungry in the kitchen.

Prayer

God who dwells in the ordinary,
Thank You for showing up in my distractions and my daily rhythms.
Even when I don't know what I'm looking for,
You meet me with grace.
Help me recognize You in the most mundane places,
Like my kitchen, my fridge, and my searching heart.
Amen.

Simple Prompt or Challenge

Every time you open the fridge this week, take one deep breath. Say a simple prayer—even one or two words, like "peace" or "Thank You." Let that moment become a micro-prayer of presence and invitation.

Optional Reflection Songs

- *Find Me at the Feet of Jesus* – Christy Nockels
- *Be My Everything* – Tim Hughes
- *Holy Spirit* – Bryan & Katie Torwalt
- *Come Near to Me* – Vineyard Worship
- *Thank You* – 7 Hills Worship

THE SACREDNESS OF REPETITION

Opening Reflection

You do it every day. Unload the dishwasher. Make the bed. Wipe the counters. Fold the laundry that will somehow be dirty again in twelve minutes.

It's easy to wonder if any of it matters. However, what if these small repetitions aren't just survival? What if they're sacred?

Scripture

"Let us not become weary in doing good, for at the proper time we will reap a harvest if we do not give up."
—Galatians 6:9 (NIV)

Devotional Thought

Faith isn't a highlight reel. It's closer to a washing machine cycle—predictable, repeated, sometimes unglamorous, but always transformative.

Repetition is where real growth happens. It's how habits form. It's how muscles are built. And it's where God often whispers, "You're becoming."

We tend to crave the extraordinary, but God works mightily in the ordinary. The same prayer whispered day after day. The same morning routine done out of love. The same meal prepared for the same little mouths. This is not failure or futility. This is faithfulness.

Even Jesus repeated Himself. He went away to pray again. He broke bread again. He forgave again. And now, through His Spirit, He meets us again—and reminds us that we are not just going in circles. We are growing in grace.

Prayer

Faithful God,
Thank You for the beauty of the routines that sustain me.
When I grow weary of doing the same things,
Remind me that You are in every moment—
Every dish washed, every diaper changed, every kind word repeated.
Teach me to embrace the sacredness of repetition
As a reflection of Your patient, persistent love.
Amen.

Simple Prompt or Challenge

Choose one repetitive task you do every day—something small and routine. Each time you do it this week, say a simple prayer of blessing for someone else in your home or life. Let repetition become intercession.

_____

_____

_____

_____

_____

_____

Optional Reflection Songs

- *Same God* – Elevation Worship
- *Do It Again* – Elevation Worship
- *Every Hour* – David Leonard
- *Even If* – MercyMe

THE LINT TRAP AND THE SOUL

Opening Reflection

You clean it out because you're supposed to—after every load. That fuzzy little net in the dryer—the lint trap—doesn't look dangerous, but if you leave it too long, things stop working, or worse, overheat.

It turns out, our souls have lint traps, too.

Scripture

> *"Create in me a clean heart,*
> *O God, and renew a right spirit within me."*
> —Psalm 51:10 (ESV)

Devotional Thought

The messes of daily life aren't treated as enemies of spiritual growth; they're metaphors for it. And the lint trap is more than a household chore. It's a mirror for the quiet buildup we ignore inside ourselves.

Little irritations. Half-processed emotions. Mental clutter. The grief we tucked away in the name of getting things done. Over time, that buildup slows us down. Our joy gets choked. Our prayers feel muffled. And we wonder why we feel heavy for no obvious reason.

God isn't mad about the buildup. He just wants to help clear it.

David's prayer in Psalm 51 is not just about repentance; it's about renewal. It's about realizing we've been carrying too much for too long and about letting God clean out the things we didn't realize were clogging our hearts.

Clearing the lint trap won't fix everything. But it helps the machine breathe. And maybe tending to our souls regularly—before things catch fire—is just as sacred.

Prayer

God who renews and restores,
Help me notice what's building up in my spirit.
Clear the places where I've grown numb or overloaded.
Teach me to pause long enough
To tend to my inner life with honesty and grace.
Thank You for not being afraid of my clutter.
You don't just tolerate me; you restore me.
Amen.

Simple Prompt or Challenge

Every time you clean the lint trap this week—or complete any small cleaning task—ask, "What am I holding onto that needs clearing?" Take five minutes to write it down or pray it out. Let cleaning your home become an act of soul care.

_____

_____

_____

_____

_____

_____

Optional Reflection Songs

- *Clear the Stage* – Jimmy Needham
- *Come Clean* – Natalie Grant
- *Clean* – Natalie Grant or Hillsong UNITED version
- *Holy Spirit, You Are Welcome Here* – Francesca Battistelli

THE UNFILTERED LIFE

Opening Reflection

There's something freeing about taking a selfie with no filter—no smoothing, no brightening, no edits. However, let's be real; it's also terrifying.

We've grown used to curating ourselves. We filter our photos, our stories, even our struggles. But God invites us to be raw, real, and beautifully unfiltered.

Scripture

> *"The Lord is near to the brokenhearted and*
> *saves the crushed in spirit."*
> —Psalm 34:18 (ESV)

Devotional Thought

Let's gently unravel the pressure to appear polished. Yes, tears may fall while stirring the soup, and laughter may escape during chaos, but we find beauty when we drop the performance and just *be*.

We live in a culture that rewards curated perfection. But faith flourishes in authenticity. God isn't looking for the version of you with perfect quiet times, color-coded planners, and emotionally neat prayer journals. He wants *you*—red-eyed, overwhelmed, doubting, joyful, honest you.

The unfiltered life is where transformation happens. When we bring God our messy feelings, our unedited thoughts, our questions that feel too raw—we're not pushed away. We're held closer.

We can stop performing. We can start breathing. God doesn't bless pretend people. He meets the real ones with compassion and closeness.

Prayer

God who sees me fully,
Thank You for not asking me to fake it.
You welcome my questions, my silence, my tears—
All of me, unfiltered.
Help me bring my real heart to You,
And teach me to extend that same grace to others.
Make my life less curated, more connected,
And beautifully real in Your hands.
Amen.

Simple Prompt or Challenge

Spend five quiet minutes journaling this week. Write down what you actually feel—not what you should feel. Then pray, "God, this is where I am. Meet me here." Let that be enough.

_____

_____

_____

_____

_____

_____

Optional Reflection Songs

- *You Already Know* – JJ Heller
- *Come Out of Hiding* – Steffany Gretzinger
- *Honest* – Francesca Battistelli
- *The Real Jesus* – JJ Weeks Band

TEARS, LAUGHTER, AND TRUTH

Opening Reflection

It's strange how quickly it happens. One minute, you're laughing until your side aches, and the next, your eyes are filled with tears you didn't know were coming.

Life is like that—joy and sorrow sharing the same breath. And maybe, just maybe, that's exactly where God lives: in the tension between the two.

Scripture

> *"There is a time for everything, and a season for every activity under the heavens . . . a time to weep and a time to laugh, a time to mourn and a time to dance."*
>
> —Ecclesiastes 3:1, 4 (NIV)

Devotional Thought

Honest emotions bubble up in ordinary moments—crying while making boxed mac and cheese, laughing in the middle of bedtime chaos, and realizing that both emotions can hold truth—and even holiness.

We tend to separate emotions into good and bad. Joy is allowed. Grief, not so much. However, the Bible doesn't split them that way. Jesus wept. Jesus rejoiced. Jesus got angry. Jesus blessed the poor in spirit and turned water into wine at a party. He was emotionally present, not emotionally perfect.

God is not asking you to clean up your feelings before coming to Him. He wants all of you. The heart that rejoices. The soul that aches. The part of you that cries in the car and the one that laughs during prayer. These aren't distractions from your faith; they're doorways into it.

The sacred life is not emotionless. It's emotionally honest. And God, full of love and compassion, is ready to meet you there.

Prayer

God of truth and tenderness,
Thank You for creating in me the capacity to feel deeply.
When I cry, let me feel Your nearness.
When I laugh, let me remember that joy is sacred, too.
Teach me to stop judging my emotions,
And instead bring them—all of them—to You.
Amen.

Simple Prompt or Challenge

Don't rush past your emotions this week. When you feel a
laugh bubbling up, let it rise. When tears come, welcome
them. At the end of each day, name one thing that made
you laugh and one thing that stirred your heart. Offer both
to God.

_____

_____

_____

_____

_____

_____

Optional Reflection Songs

- *You Say* – Lauren Daigle
- *The Blessing* – Kari Jobe & Cody Carnes
- *Through All of It* – Colton Dixon
- *Joy Invincible* – Switchfoot

THE POWER OF HONEST PRAYERS

Opening Reflection

You meant to pray something eloquent, something devotional-app worthy. But instead, what came out sounded more like, "God, I don't even know what to say right now. I'm tired. I'm overwhelmed. Help."

That's a holy prayer.

Scripture

"Before a word is on my tongue, you, Lord, know it completely."
—Psalm 139:4 (NIV)

Devotional Thought

The prayers we pray when we're wiping down the counter for the fourth time in a day are not polished or poetic. They're real—and real is enough.

Sometimes we fall into the trap of thinking prayer must be structured, scheduled, or said in a certain tone of voice. But God isn't grading our prayers. He's leaning in to hear our hearts.

Honest prayers can be messy, short, and even unfinished. They sound like, "I'm mad at You, God." Or "I want to believe, but I don't." Or even just a whispered, "Please."

These prayers carry a raw kind of power because they're true. And truth is the language of intimacy.

God doesn't want your performance. He wants your permission to come into your exhaustion, your fear, your mess, and your joy, and sit with you there. He wants to speak to you, not because you've prayed well but because you've invited Him in with whatever words you could muster.

Prayer

God who hears even the silence,
I don't always have the right words,
But I trust that You hear me anyway.
Help me let go of performing in prayer.
Give me the courage to speak honestly—
To bring You my full, unedited heart.
Thank You for receiving me with compassion every single time.
Amen.

Simple Prompt or Challenge

Set a timer for three minutes this week. Sit somewhere quiet. Speak honestly to God—no formalities, no filters, no fear. Say what's really on your heart. If all you can do is cry or sigh, let that be your prayer. He hears it all.

_____

_____

_____

_____

_____

_____

Optional Reflection Songs

- *Talk to Jesus* – Elevation Worship
- *Honest Offering* – CAIN
- *Just Be Held* – Casting Crowns
- *You Already Know* – JJ Heller
- *Hard Fought Hallelujah* – Brandon Heath & Jelly Roll

INSTAGRAM VS. INNER LIFE

Opening Reflection

Your latte is perfectly frothed. The light hits your Bible just right. You snap a picture, post it with a caption like #blessed or #quiettime—and then yell down the hall for someone to stop fighting over a sock.

It's okay. You're not fake; you're just human. But it's worth asking: is my spiritual life something I perform or something I practice?

Scripture

> *"Am I now trying to win the approval of human beings, or of God? Or am I trying to please people? If I were still trying to please people, I would not be a servant of Christ."*
> —Galatians 1:10 (NIV)

Devotional Thought

We must let go of the pressure to look like we have it all together. And nowhere is that pressure stronger than online.

Social media is a highlight reel. It's easy to craft a moment that looks holy even when we feel hollow. However, God's focus isn't on how well we curate our image; it's on how we cultivate our souls.

The danger of a performative faith is that it becomes disconnected from the messy, beautiful, authentic walk of a real relationship with God—the kind of walk that includes forgotten prayers, rushed mornings, and spiritually dry seasons.

There's nothing wrong with beautiful Bible pages or shared encouragement online. But the heart work—that happens when no one is watching. That's where transformation is born.

We don't need to impress God. We just need to invite Him into the parts we post and the parts we hide.

Prayer

God who sees beyond the filters,
Thank You for loving me in full color—flaws, fatigue, and all.
Help me nurture my soul,
Not just my image.

Teach me to be honest, real, and rooted in You.
Strip away performance and replace it with presence.
Amen.

Simple Prompt or Challenge

Take a break from curating. This week, spend one devotional time without posting about it. Just be present. Then, ask yourself honestly: *What is my inner life saying right now?* Jot down one phrase or word that captures that truth and talk to God about it.

_____

_____

_____

_____

_____

_____

Optional Reflection Songs

- *Inside Out* – Hillsong UNITED
- *You See Me* – Christy Nockels
- *Run to the Father* – Cody Carnes
- *The Real Jesus* – JJ Weeks Band

WHEN YOU CAN'T REACH THE STARS

Opening Reflection

You had dreams once—big ones. You had visions of what life would look like, what success would feel like, what faith would feel like if you ever really "got there."

However, here you are: tired, overdue on the oil change, Googling "easy chicken dishes," and wondering if you're doing this whole life thing right. The stars feel far.

But maybe you weren't meant to reach the stars. Maybe you were meant to stand at the counter and be found.

Scripture

> *"The Lord makes firm the steps of the one who delights in him; though he may stumble, he will not fall, for the Lord upholds him with his hand."*
> —Psalm 37:23–24 (NIV)

Devotional Thought

It's time to push back on the cultural obsession with extraordinary living, with chasing the stars. Sometimes what we really need isn't to aim higher; it's to go deeper.

There's nothing wrong with ambition. But when it starts to measure our worth, crush our joy, or disconnect us from the sacred beauty of the life right in front of us, it's no longer holy; it's heavy.

You don't need to launch something big to live a meaningful life. Some of the most sacred work you'll ever do will happen without fanfare. It'll be in the pickup line, at the kitchen table, or while holding a hurting friend's hand.

God isn't asking you to dazzle. He's asking you to dwell with Him, with your people, in this moment. Right here is enough. You are enough.

Prayer

God of grounded grace,
Thank You for not measuring my worth by my
accomplishments.
When I feel like I'm falling short,
Remind me that You delight in my presence—not my
performance.
Help me to lay down the dream of being amazing
And pick up the peace of being faithful.
Amen.

Simple Prompt or Challenge

Write down one star you've been reaching for—a dream, expectation, or standard that's weighing you down. Cross it out and underneath, write: "Faithfulness in the ordinary is enough." Place it where you'll see it this week.

_____

_____

_____

_____

_____

_____

Optional Reflection Songs

- *Dream Small* – Josh Wilson
- *Altogether Good* – Citizens
- *You Already Know* – JJ Heller
- *Be Still and Know* – Steven Curtis Chapman
- *Quiet* – Hillside Recording

WONDER OVER ACHIEVEMENT

Opening Reflection

Some days you achieve. You finish the to-do list, remember the lunchboxes, and even fold the laundry before it wrinkles.

However, other days, you stare at the sky. You notice the shimmer of soap bubbles in the sink. You laugh at something small and silly. Nothing got finished, but your soul exhaled.

And maybe that's the bigger win.

Scripture

> *"The Lord will fight for you; you need only to be still."*
> —Exodus 14:14 (NIV)

Devotional Thought

Life isn't a competition to be won; it's a wonder to be noticed. Somewhere along the way, we began believing that our days only matter if they're productive, that worth is earned through output, and that being still is wasting time.

However, wonder rewrites that narrative. It tells us that simply being here—awake, aware, breathing—is more than enough. Wonder isn't passive. It's powerful. It pulls us into presence, deepens our joy, and invites us to meet God in the now.

Children live this way. They marvel at puddles. They examine bugs. They don't ask if they're being useful; they just are. Jesus says that kind of faith—the childlike kind—is the key to the kingdom.

Instead of reaching for the next accomplishment, try reaching for a moment of awe. Let wonder interrupt your day. Let it remind you that you are already living something holy.

Prayer

God of wonder and slow beauty,
Quiet the voice that tells me to do more, be more, prove more.
Awaken me to the small miracles around me—
The breath in my lungs, the rhythm of grace, the sacred in the ordinary.
Let me choose awe over anxiety,
Stillness over striving,
And wonder over worry.
Amen.

Simple Prompt or Challenge

Go on a ten-minute wonder walk. No phone. No agenda. Just walk and notice. Name five beautiful things out loud— no matter how small. Let each one be a moment of worship.

_____

_____

_____

_____

_____

_____

Optional Reflection Songs

- *So Will I (100 Billion X)* – Hillsong UNITED
- *Wonderfully Made* – Ellie Holcomb
- *Quiet* – Hillside Recording
- *This Is the Day* – The Porter's Gate
- *Beautiful Things* – Gungor

THE ENOUGH LIFE

Opening Reflection

You didn't do it all. The house is still a mess. The thing you meant to say, fix, or send is still undone. You feel behind, maybe even inadequate.

But here's the truth: You are not the sum of your accomplishments. You are already enough because grace says so.

Scripture

> *"My flesh and my heart may fail, but God is the strength of my heart and my portion forever."*
> —Psalm 73:26 (NIV)

Devotional Thought

Perhaps we should acknowledge the exhausting pressure to be amazing, chase the stars, and prove our worth through hustle or highlight reels. The invitation God offers is simpler, deeper, and far more freeing: *Be faithful. Be present. Be held.*

The enough life isn't flashy. It's rooted.

It shows up in quiet trust instead of loud effort. In choosing rest when the world pushes for more. In believing God is more interested in who you are becoming than in what you're checking off.

Living the enough life means accepting that the unfinished parts of your day—or your heart—don't disqualify you. They simply create space for God's power to be visible. It's not about arriving at perfection. It's about learning to rest in sufficiency.

Because grace never says, "Try harder."
It says, "Come closer."

Prayer

God of enough,
Help me to live from rest, not striving,
To believe that I am loved as I am—
Even when I fall short, even when I forget.
Quiet the voice of pressure,
And let me hear only Your invitation:
"You are mine. You are enough. Come rest."
Amen.

Simple Prompt or Challenge

Write this truth on a sticky note or your bathroom mirror: "I don't have to be more. I am enough in God's grace today." Read it aloud every morning this week. Let it become your breath prayer.

_____

_____

_____

_____

_____

_____

Optional Reflection Songs

- *Jireh* – Maverick City Music
- *Enough* – BarlowGirl
- *You Are More* – Tenth Avenue North
- *I Am* – Crowder
- *I Will Trust* – Red Rocks Worship

EMBRACING JUST OKAY DAYS

Opening Reflection

Today wasn't terrible, but it wasn't great either. You didn't conquer the world. You didn't melt down. You got the dishwasher unloaded, remembered to eat lunch, and maybe wore real pants.

That's it. Nothing to post on Instagram. Just okay. And you know what? That's beautiful.

Scripture

> *"Give us this day our daily bread."*
> —Matthew 6:11 (ESV)

Devotional Thought

Not every day needs to be remarkable to be meaningful. Some days are simply steady, plain, and repetitive. They don't make headlines, but they quietly hold the fabric of our lives together.

Our culture doesn't celebrate just okay days. We're trained to crave highs, breakthroughs, and mountaintop moments. But God shows up in the valleys, in the quiet, in the perfectly average Tuesday when nothing grand happened except that you lived it faithfully.

Jesus taught us to pray for daily bread—not weekly blessings or annual miracles. Just what we need, today. That means we're invited to trust God not just in the big decisions or emotional highs but in the neutral hours, too. He's just as present on the okay days as He is on the breathtaking ones.

So, if you're in a season of neutral, take heart. Faith isn't a highlight reel; it's a quiet walk with a present God. And He calls these just okay days "good."

Prayer

Faithful God,
Thank You for the days that are quiet and steady.
Teach me to stop measuring my worth by how exciting my life feels.
Help me find peace in the normal,
Joy in the ordinary,
And You in the middle of it all.
Amen.

Simple Prompt or Challenge

At the end of today, write down three just okay things that happened—a simple meal, a task you finished, a conversation, a breath. Name them. Give thanks for them. Let the ordinary become your offering.

_____

_____

_____

_____

_____

_____

Optional Reflection Songs

- *Daily Bread* – United Pursuit
- *Simple Things* – Sandra McCracken
- *Every Little Thing* – Hillsong Young & Free
- *Still* – Amanda Lindsey Cook
- *I Will Trust* – Red Rocks Worship

PART IV

STANDING TALL
(ON THE COUNTER)

GRATITUDE IN THE GROCERY LINE

Opening Reflection

It starts with a cart that has a squeaky wheel and a line that's moving slower than your toddler gets dressed. You check your watch. You huff a little. You scroll mindlessly. It's just a grocery line; what could possibly be sacred here?

Plenty.

Scripture

> *"Give thanks in all circumstances;*
> *for this is God's will for you in Christ Jesus."*
> —1 Thessalonians 5:18 (NIV)

Devotional Thought

The sacred isn't saved for Sunday. It's tucked into the corners of everyday life, even in Aisle 7 between the canned soup and clearance cereal—especially there.

Gratitude is less about our circumstances and more about our awareness. Most of life isn't lived on mountaintops; it's lived in errands, waiting rooms, and grocery store lines. And these moments offer a holy invitation: *to see*.

To see the child dancing to the overhead music.
To notice the elderly woman carefully counting coupons.
To offer a smile instead of a sigh.
To breathe and say, "Thank You for this day, this food, this ordinary mercy."

The grocery line can become a sacred altar if you let it.

Gratitude isn't about feeling grateful; it's about choosing to look, even when you're hungry and tired and your cart won't stop veering left.

Prayer

God of ordinary places,
Open my eyes to Your presence in the slow lines, the quiet moments,
The spaces where I least expect to find You.
Give me a heart that notices goodness,
Even when I feel rushed or restless.
Teach me to choose gratitude—
Right here, right now, with this cart and this breath.
Amen.

Simple Prompt or Challenge

This week, while you're standing in a line—at the store, at a stoplight, in the school pickup—pause. Breathe. Look around. Silently name three things you're grateful for. Let a slow moment become a sacred one.

_____

_____

_____

_____

_____

_____

Optional Reflection Songs

- *Gratitude* – Brandon Lake
- *Every Good Thing* – The Afters
- *Simple Kingdom* – Bryan & Katie Torwalt
- *Count Every Blessing* – Rend Collective

DEEP BREATHS AND BUGGIES

Opening Reflection

You're halfway through the grocery store. One kid is asking for cereal shaped like dinosaurs, your phone just died, and your cart (or "buggy," depending on where you live) has developed a mind of its own.

You pause. You inhale deeply—not because everything is peaceful but because you desperately need peace to find you.

Scripture

> *"The Lord gives strength to his people;*
> *the Lord blesses his people with peace."*
> —Psalm 29:11 (NIV)

Devotional Thought

Our goal isn't a flawless life. It's a faithful one. And sometimes the most faithful thing you can do is take a breath between frozen pizza and peanut butter, look around, and whisper, "God, I'm here. Are You?"

Spoiler alert: He is.

Peace isn't the absence of motion; it's the presence of God in the middle of it. It's learning to breathe with intention when life feels anything but calm. It's choosing to respond with grace instead of grumbling, even when your list is long and the toddler is loud.

Jesus didn't only walk through quiet gardens. He walked through crowds—busy, messy, unpredictable places. And He remained centered, rooted, and present. That same peace He carried is available to you, even when your buggy keeps veering into the cracker display.

Prayer

Jesus,
Meet me in the middle of the chaos—
In crowded aisles and cluttered thoughts.
Slow my breath, quiet my mind,
And remind me that peace is not found in a perfect day
But in Your perfect presence,
Even here, even now.
Amen.

Simple Prompt or Challenge

This week, practice a peace pause during a busy moment (grocery store, school pickup, work stress). Place your hand over your heart and take a deep breath. Inhale: "You are with me." Exhale: "I am at peace." Repeat as needed.

_____

_____

_____

_____

_____

_____

Optional Reflection Songs

- *Breathe* – Jonny Diaz
- *Peace Be Still* – Hope Darst
- *It Is Well (Through It All)* – Kristene DiMarco
- *The World Needs Jesus* – We the Kingdom
- *Found* – Amanda Cook

THE HOLINESS OF SMALL TALK

Opening Reflection

"How's it going?"
"Busy. You?"
"Can you believe this weather?"

We often breeze through these familiar lines, eyes already shifting to our phones or our next errand. But what if these tiny, forgettable moments are full of holy potential?

Scripture

> *"Let your conversation be always full of grace, seasoned with salt, so that you may know how to answer everyone."*
> —Colossians 4:6 (NIV)

Devotional Thought

We can all find meaning, not just in grand gestures or profound conversations but in the humble, habitual moments of connection. That brief comment to the cashier. The light-hearted joke with the mail carrier. The "How's your mom doing?" to a neighbor passing by.

We tend to dismiss small talk as insignificant. But kindness is never wasted. Every interaction is an opportunity to bring presence—to plant peace, speak grace, or simply remind someone that they matter.

Jesus had deep conversations, yes. But He also asked every-day questions. He noticed people. He turned ordinary meals and water-fetching into moments of transformation.

When we slow down enough to look people in the eye—even for just a few seconds—we reflect the very heart of God: the One who always sees, always listens, always loves.

Prayer

God of daily moments,
Help me not to overlook the small spaces—
The ordinary greetings, the casual encounters.
Let my words be grace-filled and intentional,
Even in the briefest of conversations.
Teach me to listen well and love fully,
One interaction at a time.
Amen.

Simple Prompt or Challenge

This week, be intentionally present in at least one moment of small talk. Ask a thoughtful follow-up question. Smile with your eyes. Remember a name. Let someone know they were truly seen, even in a brief exchange.

_____

_____

_____

_____

_____

_____

Optional Reflection Songs

- *Speak Life* – TobyMac
- *Let Them See You* – JJ Weeks Band
- *With Every Act of Love* – Jason Gray
- *Love God, Love People* – Danny Gokey

HOPE WITH A SIDE OF DISHES

Opening Reflection

You didn't expect to cry while unloading the dishwasher—but there you were. Somewhere between the spoons and cereal bowls, the weight of everything caught up with you.

Life didn't fall apart. It just piled up—again. And all you could do was rinse, breathe, and hope that God saw you. He did.

Scripture

> *"Let us hold unswervingly to the hope we profess, for he who promised is faithful."*
> —Hebrews 10:23 (NIV)

Devotional Thought

The divine doesn't wait for things to be quiet and tidy. God meets us in the messy middle—between school drop-offs, unpaid bills, unfinished prayers, and, yes, the dishes.

Hope isn't always bright and confident. Sometimes it's whispered through gritted teeth. Sometimes it's the choice to wash the dishes while your heart aches. Sometimes it means just showing up.

But here's what matters: Hope doesn't have to be loud to be real. It only has to endure. And the One who holds your hope is faithful—whether you feel strong or not.

So, if your prayers feel repetitive, your days feel small, and your faith feels like a flickering candle, don't panic. That little light still counts. God still counts it. He's not asking you to shine like a spotlight. He's only asking you to keep showing up with your hands in the sink and your heart still hoping.

Prayer

God of slow faith and silent strength,
Thank You for meeting me in the middle of my ordinary.
When my hope feels fragile, hold it for me.
When life feels repetitive, remind me that You are still working.
Help me cling to You, even when all I have left is a whisper.
You are faithful. You are near.
And that is enough.
Amen.

Simple Prompt or Challenge

Choose one everyday task this week—washing dishes, folding laundry, sweeping the floor—and turn it into a prayer of hope. As you do the work, say aloud: "I'm still here, Lord. I still believe." Let your hands speak what your heart may be struggling to say.

_____

_____

_____

_____

_____

_____

Optional Reflection Songs

- *Even If* – MercyMe
- *Hold On to Me* – Lauren Daigle
- *Keep Me in the Moment* – Jeremy Camp
- *Hope Has a Name* – Passion Music

BEAUTY IN BROKEN PLACES

Opening Reflection

You didn't mean to have a breakdown; you just dropped a plate. Cracked it clean in half. And suddenly, it felt like more than a dish. It felt like your hope, your plans, your heart.

However, as you stared at the brokenness, something sacred whispered: "This isn't the end. It's the beginning of something new."

Scripture

> *"He heals the brokenhearted and binds up their wounds."*
> —Psalm 147:3 (NIV)

Devotional Thought

Beauty doesn't only rise from picture-perfect moments. Sometimes it grows slowly, stubbornly, and through the cracks.

We all have broken places—moments when life did not go as planned, when grief came uninvited, when dreams dissolved quietly. And yet, in those places, God begins the kind of work that can't be manufactured—only "miracled."

Kintsugi is a Japanese art form that repairs broken pottery with gold. It doesn't hide the cracks; it highlights them. It makes them part of the story. That's what God does with us. He doesn't discard our brokenness. He redeems it. And when we surrender our shattered parts, He creates something more beautiful than before.

Don't fear the broken places in your life. That's often where healing begins. That's where grace shows up with golden light and says, "I can work with this."

Prayer

God of restoration,
You don't run from brokenness; You run toward it.
Take the parts of me that feel cracked, weary, or hopeless,
And bind them with grace.
Help me to believe that You can make beauty from my pain,
Light from my shadows, and purpose from my past.
Thank You for not needing perfection—only surrender.
Amen.

Simple Prompt or Challenge

Find a broken item in your home—a chipped mug, a cracked plate, a worn item of clothing. Don't throw it away. Instead, let it remind you that God doesn't discard what is broken. He transforms it. Write one way God has brought (or is bringing) beauty from a hard season.

_____

_____

_____

_____

_____

_____

Optional Reflection Songs

- *Broken Vessels (Amazing Grace)* – Hillsong Worship
- *Beauty for Ashes* – Crystal Lewis
- *Mended* – Matthew West
- *God Turn It Around* – Jon Reddick
- *Beautiful Things* - Gungor

WHEN FAITH FEELS BORING

Opening Reflection

You sit down to pray, and your mind drifts to the grocery list. You open your Bible and reread the same paragraph three times. Sunday feels like a routine. Quiet time feels like background noise.

You love God. You really do. But your faith feels kind of boring.

Scripture

"Let us run with perseverance the race marked out for us, fixing our eyes on Jesus, the pioneer and perfecter of faith."
—Hebrews 12:1-2 (ESV)

Devotional Thought

The sacredness of repetition—of showing up when it's not exciting—is honored as one of the truest expressions of faith.

We often associate faith with passion, revival, and emotion. And yes, those moments matter. However, real faith often looks like quiet consistency, like praying even when you don't feel it, like opening your Bible when it doesn't give you goosebumps, and like folding laundry while whispering, "I trust You."

Think of a long, faithful marriage. It's not built on fireworks every day. It's built on choosing to stay, choosing to love, and choosing to be present.

Faith is the same. It is formed not only in the powerful moments but also in the patient ones. In the boring ones. In the days when we say, "I'm here, God," and that's the best we've got.

And that is beautiful.

Prayer

God of steady presence,
Thank You for not requiring my faith to be flashy.
When I feel dry, distracted, or disconnected,
Draw me back gently to You.
Remind me that showing up matters,
That my devotion isn't measured by emotion
But by the willingness to stay near You,
Even in the quiet.
Amen.

Simple Prompt or Challenge

This week, choose one spiritual practice. Read a Psalm, pray aloud, or simply sit in silence. Do it for five minutes each day, even if you feel nothing. At the end of the week, write down one small way you sensed God's presence before, during, or after.

_____

_____

_____

_____

_____

_____

Optional Reflection Songs

- *Faithful Now* – Vertical Worship
- *Still* – Amanda Lindsey Cook
- *Even If* – MercyMe
- *Great Is Thy Faithfulness* – Shane & Shane
- *I Will Trust* – Red Rocks Worship
- *Psalm 23* – Phil Wickham

THE COUNTER IS ENOUGH

Opening Reflection

The counter catches everything: lunch crumbs, backpacks, unopened mail, elbow marks, grocery bags, half-finished prayers. It's not glamorous, but it's where life happens.

And maybe, just maybe, it's where holiness happens, too.

Scripture

> *"But godliness with contentment is great gain."*
> —1 Timothy 6:6 (NIV)

Devotional Thought

Do you think we've been reaching for the wrong things? While the world tells us to reach for the stars—achievement, recognition, perfection—Jesus invites us to reach for something closer. Something steadier. Something like a kitchen counter.

That countertop is a symbol of daily faith—not flashy, but faithful. A surface where grace is served on paper plates, prayers are whispered through dishwater, and little miracles are stacked between the bananas and the bills.

You don't need to aim higher to matter more. You don't need to be more extraordinary to be more loved. The counter—the real one in your actual kitchen—is enough. Because you are enough. And God is already present there, in the ordinary, offering sacred presence in everyday moments.

Let the counter remind you that you're not behind. You're not too small. You are deeply seen, deeply known, and deeply loved.

Prayer

God of the sacred ordinary,
Thank You for meeting me at the counter—
Where life is cluttered, noisy, and beautiful.
Help me stop reaching for unreachable expectations
And start embracing the holiness right in front of me.
Let contentment be my posture
And presence be my gift.
Amen.

Simple Prompt or Challenge

Clear a small space on your kitchen counter. Place something simple and sacred there this week—a candle, a cross,
a prayer card. Let it be your physical reminder: "God meets
me here. This is enough."

_____

_____

_____

_____

_____

_____

Optional Reflection Songs

- *Altogether Good* – Citizens
- *Jireh* – Maverick City Music
- *Good Enough* – Coby James
- *Here Again* – Elevation Worship

RICH, SIMPLE, AND REAL

Opening Reflection

You may not have a dream kitchen, a bucket list vacation, or a social calendar that screams success. But you have tea in a chipped mug, laughter in the hallway, a dog that sheds too much, and people who know your weird quirks and love you anyway.

That's not lacking. That's abundance.

Scripture

> *"Better a little with the fear of the Lord*
> *than great wealth with turmoil."*
> —Proverbs 15:16 (NIV)

Devotional Thought

Let's redefine what richness really means. Because in a culture that glorifies hustle, status, and accumulation, the counter life offers something wildly countercultural: *"enoughness."*

There's richness in the simplicity of a shared meal. There's wealth in the sound of a child's laugh, the rhythm of routine, the ability to exhale. A life of deep roots, quiet moments, and honest conversations doesn't make headlines, but it makes a difference.

God's economy has always flipped ours upside-down. The poor in spirit inherit the kingdom. The meek inherit the earth. The last will be first. So don't discount your life if it doesn't look big. If it's rich in love, grace, patience, and truth, you are living abundantly.

You don't need more to be full. You need less noise, more presence. Less performance, more truth. Less striving, more stillness.

Simple. Sacred. Enough.

Prayer

God of contentment and quiet joy,
Thank You for the richness of my right-now life.
Help me recognize wealth not by what I have,
But by the love that surrounds me,
The grace that carries me,
And the truth that sets me free.
Teach me to embrace a life that is
Rich, simple, and real.
Amen.

Simple Prompt or Challenge

Make a gratitude list this week of simple riches in your life—things that don't cost anything but make your soul feel full. Post it somewhere visible and revisit it each morning. Let it anchor your heart in real abundance. (Try dry-erase markers on your bathroom mirror!)

_____

_____

_____

_____

_____

_____

Optional Reflection Songs

- *Simple Kingdom* – Bryan & Katie Torwalt
- *Goodness of God* – CeCe Winans
- *Satisfied* – Jordan Feliz
- *Give Me Jesus* – Fernando Ortega

Week 45

THE DAILY REACH

Opening Reflection

You reach for a drinking glass, a lunchbox, a lost sock, your patience—again.

You reach dozens of times a day without even thinking. But what if each reach could become a reminder? A small spiritual practice that says, "God, I want to meet You here in this moment, in this mess, in this stretch of grace."

Scripture

> *"Come near to God and he will come near to you."*
> —James 4:8a (NIV)

Devotional Thought

The message is clear: You don't need to chase the stars to live a meaningful, spiritual life. The invitation isn't up and out; it's here and in. It's in the counter, the quiet, the real, the reachable.

Every day is full of tiny moments of reaching:

- Reaching for peace when your nerves are frayed
- Reaching for kindness when sarcasm feels easier
- Reaching for hope when headlines weigh heavily
- Reaching for truth when comparison whispers lies
- Reaching for God—not in a big, impressive way—but in a small, honest one

That's what faith looks like most of the time—not leaps but reaches. Reaching for something just outside your comfort zone but within God's grace. And He meets us there every single time.

Prayer

God of gentle grace,
Teach me to reach for You today—
In small ways, in quiet moments, in ordinary routines.
Let every stretch of my heart be met by Your presence.
Help me choose faith not by climbing higher,
But by leaning closer.
You are always within reach,
And for that, I'm so grateful.
Amen.

Simple Prompt or Challenge

Every time you physically reach for something this week—
your coffee, your phone, your child's hand—whisper a
prayer: "Lord, I reach for You in this moment." Let this
be your breath prayer and grounding reminder throughout
the day.

_____

_____

_____

_____

_____

_____

Optional Reflection Songs

- *Reach Out* – Influencers Worship
- *Here's My Heart* – Lauren Daigle
- *Draw Me Close* – Michael W. Smith
- *Closer* – Lifepoint Worship

LIVING THE COUNTER LIFE

Opening Reflection

You didn't have a mountaintop moment today. You didn't achieve world peace or finish the laundry. But you did show up. You made meals. You answered texts. You folded half a basket of towels and sheets.

It may not have looked like much. But it was holy. This is the counter life.

Scripture

> *"Make it your ambition to lead a quiet life: You should mind your own business and work with your hands . . ."*
> —1 Thessalonians 4:11 (NIV)

Devotional Thought

The counter life is not a small life. It's a faithful life—a life built not on highlight reels but on honest rhythms. It's a life where grace is practiced in silence, in sweat, and in steady acts of love that go unnoticed by the world but not by God.

To live the counter life is to resist the pressure to hustle, impress, and achieve endlessly. It's to say, "I don't need to reach for the stars to be significant. I will reach for the counter and find that God is already there."

This life is rooted in presence. In slow mornings. In ordinary prayers. In the sacred act of sitting down with your people, offering love with tired eyes and full hearts.

Living the counter life means waking up to what's already here. It means knowing your small moments are seen. Your quiet faith is enough. Your ordinary offerings are holy.

This is not second-best. It is sacred. It is full. It is real life.

Prayer

Lord of the ordinary,
Help me embrace the counter life—
The grounded, grace-filled, sacredly simple way of living.
Teach me to show up with love,
To serve with joy,
And to find beauty in what the world might call "small."
Let my daily life reflect Your steady presence.
Amen.

Simple Prompt or Challenge

Make a short list this week titled "This Is My Counter Life."
Include small acts of love, grace, or presence you practice
regularly (making lunch, sending kind texts, praying while
folding laundry). Hang it somewhere visible. Let it remind
you that you are already living a life that matters.

_____

_____

_____

_____

_____

_____

Optional Reflection Songs

- *This Is the Stuff* – Francesca Battistelli
- *Little Things With Great Love* – Audrey Assad
- *To Be Loved* – Nichole Nordeman
- *Living Hope* – Phil Wickham

THE ORDINARY WAY IS THE HOLY WAY

Opening Reflection

We expect to find God on mountaintops, in revival meetings, and in perfectly lit quiet times with instrumental music playing in the background.

However, holiness doesn't just live in the grand. It lives in the grit, the grocery lists, the morning breath prayers, and the sink full of last night's dishes.

And maybe that's not a downgrade. Maybe that's the design.

Scripture

> *"Your word is a lamp to my feet and a light to my path."*
> —Psalm 119:105 (NIV)

Devotional Thought

This is a sacred truth: God is not waiting for you to arrive somewhere more impressive. He's walking with you through the ordinary because the ordinary is the way.

The lamp God gives in Psalm 119 doesn't light up the whole mountain; it lights the next step. Faith isn't a spotlight on our achievements. It's a slow, steady glow on our path. And most days, that path looks like errands and carpool lines and answering emails with a little more kindness than you feel.

Jesus Himself lived this way. He cooked fish. He walked dusty roads. He spoke in stories about seeds and bread and lamps. He chose the ordinary, not as a backdrop to holiness but as the very setting of it.

You don't need to escape your life to be close to God. You only need to walk with Him in it. One faithful step at a time.

Prayer

Jesus,
Thank You for not asking me to impress You—
Only to walk with You.
Remind me that my ordinary life
Is not an obstacle to holiness;
It is the path.
Help me see each small act
As a sacred step with You.
Amen.

Simple Prompt or Challenge

Write out a litany of your ordinary. List the simple, daily tasks you'll do today: make coffee, answer messages, feed someone, clean something. Beside each, write: "This is holy when done with You." Read it aloud as your morning blessing.

_____

_____

_____

_____

_____

_____

Optional Reflection Songs

- *Thy Word* – Amy Grant & Michael W. Smith
- *Word of God Speak* – MercyMe
- *Ordinary Ways* – Sandra McCracken

CONTENTMENT IN THE CUPBOARDS

Opening Reflection

You open the pantry and sigh. There's food, but nothing fun—no gourmet sauces, no recipe inspiration, just rice, some old soup, and a box of cereal you forgot you bought.

It's not a feast. But maybe it's enough. Maybe it's exactly what grace looks like in a cupboard.

Scripture

> "I have learned the secret of being content in any and every situation . . . whether well fed or hungry, whether living in plenty or in want."
>
> —Philippians 4:12 (NIV)

Devotional Thought

Joy is not the result of abundance. It's the fruit of awareness. The cupboard doesn't have to overflow to hold enough. Sometimes, it holds just enough—and that's where gratitude begins.

We are taught to want more—better snacks, fancier dinners, fuller carts. But contentment starts when we say, "This is what I have, and this is good. This will nourish me," not just physically but spiritually.

Because contentment isn't complacency, it's clarity. It's looking at the rice and beans and realizing you're fed, looking at your ordinary life and realizing it's full of extraordinary grace.

God has a way of multiplying what looks small. And sometimes, the miracle isn't that the food stretches; it's that your peace deepens.

Prayer

God of every cupboard and craving,
Thank You for what I have—
Even when it's simple, even when it's less than flashy.
Help me find peace in provision,
Gratitude in the plain,
And joy in enough.
Amen.

Simple Prompt or Challenge

Open your pantry or fridge this week and say aloud, "Thank You for this. This is enough today." Then prepare a simple meal with what you have—intentionally, slowly, with gratitude. Let it become a quiet celebration of God's daily provision.

_____

_____

_____

_____

_____

_____

Optional Reflection Songs

- *Enough* – BarlowGirl
- *Give Me Jesus* – Fernando Ortega
- *Simple Things* – Christy Nockels
- *You're All I Need* – Hillsong Worship

A QUIET YES TO TODAY

Opening Reflection

There's always something pulling us toward *later*. Later, when things calm down. Later, when you feel more inspired. Later, when you're better, stronger, and ready.

But God doesn't ask you to be ready for later. He just asks for a quiet "yes" to today.

Scripture

> *"This is the day that the Lord has made;*
> *let us rejoice and be glad in it."*
> —Psalm 118:24 (ESV)

Devotional Thought

Holiness is not found in the perfect future we imagine. It's found in the imperfect present we often resist.

It's tempting to wish this day away, to wait for a better version of yourself or a clearer plan, or just a little more motivation. But today—the one with dishes and unanswered emails and tired eyes—is the one God made. And it's worth showing up for.

You don't have to do everything today. You don't have to feel amazing today. You just need to say yes to what's in front of you. Yes to God's presence in it. Yes to His strength instead of your own. Yes to small faith, quiet obedience, and gentle kindness.

That quiet yes is how a faithful life is built—one whisper at a time.

Prayer

God of this moment,
I don't have to know what's next—
I just have to say yes to now.
So here it is:
Yes to loving with what I have.
Yes to trusting even when I'm uncertain.
Yes to You, here, now, in this unglamorous and holy day.
Amen.

Simple Prompt or Challenge

Each morning this week, before your feet hit the floor, whisper, "Yes, Lord—just for today." Then live with gentle openness to whatever the day brings, trusting that your small yes is more than enough for God to work with.

_____

_____

_____

_____

_____

_____

Optional Reflection Songs

- *Yes I Will* – Vertical Worship
- *This Is the Day* – The Porter's Gate
- *Here I Am* – Downhere
- *Daily Bread* – United Pursuit
- *I Will Trust* – Red Rocks Worship

PART V

REACHING FURTHER

Week 50

THE VIEW FROM THE COUNTER

Opening Reflection

It's not a mountaintop, but you can see a lot from here.

The kitchen counter may not look impressive. It's seen spills, bills, elbow marks, and half-finished homework. However, it's also held joy, laughter, prayers, quiet strength, and grace poured out in invisible ways.

The view from here is beautiful.

Scripture

> *"Taste and see that the Lord is good;*
> *blessed is the one who takes refuge in him."*
> —Psalm 34:8 (NIV)

Devotional Thought

The counter is more than a simple kitchen surface. It's a symbol of real life—daily, messy, reliable. It's where truth gets lived out in ordinary faithfulness, not spiritual fireworks. And now, nearly a year into this journey, you see the sacred patterns emerging from all those seemingly simple days.

The counter has taught us that:

- Beauty lives in repetition.
- Holiness doesn't need a spotlight.
- Joy can be found in socks, cereal, and soul-deep sighs.
- God isn't distant. He's at eye level—present, here.

The view from the counter isn't always grand, but it's true. You see love practiced, not just professed. You see grace show up in familiar faces and tasks. You see a God who doesn't demand your perfection but delights in your presence.

So, when life feels just okay, when you're tempted to aim higher, do more, be more—pause. Look around. This view is enough. And God is in it.

Prayer

God of kitchen counters and quiet moments,
Thank You for all I've seen from this place—
The beauty, the grief, the grace that lingers in the ordinary.
Help me keep noticing, keep breathing,
Keep finding You right where I am.
Let this counter—this life—
Be a place of worship, wisdom, and wonder.
Amen.

Simple Prompt or Challenge

Sit at your kitchen counter (or a space that symbolizes daily life for you). Make a list titled "What I've Seen from Here." List everything from spiritual lessons to funny memories to small graces. Let it become a song of gratitude for the real, raw beauty of the everyday.

_____

_____

_____

_____

_____

_____

Optional Reflection Songs

- *The Goodness* – TobyMac & Blessing Offor
- *Take It All In* – Group 1 Crew
- *You've Already Won* – Shane & Shane
- *Great Are You Lord* – All Sons & Daughters

A FINAL LAUGH, A DEEP BREATH

Opening Reflection

You overbaked the brownies. Forgot the appointment. Found the missing sock in the fridge. You cried over nothing and laughed inappropriately in serious moments.

Congratulations. You are fully alive.

And if you're not laughing—even a little—you might be missing the holiness in humanity.

Scripture

> *"She is clothed with strength and dignity;*
> *she can laugh at the days to come."*
> —Proverbs 31:25 (NIV)

Devotional Thought

Humor isn't just a narrative tool; it's a spiritual one. It reminds us not to take ourselves too seriously, that God isn't offended by our awkwardness, and that grace holds us through tears and laughter.

Faith without joy is fragile. But faith that learns to chuckle—even through tears—is deeply rooted. Why? Because laughter requires presence. It invites humility. It recognizes we are not in control—and lets that be a gift instead of a threat.

Jesus didn't avoid messy people. He didn't flinch at human moments. He reclined at tables, welcomed little ones, and used humor in His stories. If the Savior of the world made room for laughter, so can we.

So, exhale. Smile, even when things don't go as planned—especially then.

Sometimes the most sacred thing you can do is laugh and let yourself be loved right there.

Prayer

God of grace and giggles,
Thank You for the gift of laughter—
For the absurd, the unexpected, the wonderfully human.
Help me not to take myself too seriously
But to walk in joy,
To breathe deep,
And to remember that Your love makes space for humor,
Even in the holiest places.
Amen.

Simple Prompt or Challenge

Do one thing this week purely for the joy of it: watch a funny movie, retell an old inside joke, send a ridiculous meme. As you laugh, whisper this prayer, **"Thank You, God, for being present in my joy."** Let laughter become your worship.

_____

_____

_____

_____

_____

_____

Optional Reflection Songs

- *Joy* – Rend Collective
- *Grace Wins* – Matthew West
- *Laugh Out Loud* – Jason Gray
- *Alive & Breathing* – Matt Maher

Week 52

YOU WERE ALWAYS ENOUGH

Opening Reflection

Maybe you didn't finish every devotional in this book. Some weeks, you rushed. Others you cried. Some days, you forgot to pray, and other days, you whispered prayers you didn't think God wanted to hear.

However, here you are—still showing up, still breathing, still reaching.

You were never supposed to be perfect—just present.

You are beloved.

Scripture

> *"See, I have engraved you on the palms of my hands."*
> —Isaiah 49:16a (NIV)

Devotional Thought

After a year of leaning into the ordinary, embracing the mess, and meeting God in the crumbs and laundry piles, the truth rises: this entire time—on your best days and your most undone ones—you were already enough.

Not because you made progress. Not because you got more organized or spiritually productive. But because *God never needed you to prove yourself.* He only asked for your presence.

You've reached for the counter. And what you found wasn't a smaller life; it was a sacred one—rooted, real, and laced with joy, pain, humor, fatigue, worship, and wonder.

The most beautiful part is that sacred life was already yours—even before you began this devotional, even before the first prayer was whispered. You didn't become enough. You remembered that you already are.

You are deeply known, deeply seen, and deeply loved.

Not because you reached high but because you allowed God to meet you down low.

Prayer

God of final words and fresh beginnings,
Thank You for walking with me
In every messy, mundane, and miraculous moment.
Remind me, again and again,

That I don't have to become more to be more.
I am already enough because I am Yours.
Let that truth rest in my bones,
Shape my days,
And soften my striving.
Amen.

Simple Prompt or Challenge

Write a letter to yourself from one year ago. Be kind. Be honest. Remind that version of you what you've learned about love, presence, grace, and worth. Seal it in your journal or email it to yourself to review next year.

_____

_____

_____

_____

_____

_____

Optional Reflection Songs

- *You Say* – Lauren Daigle
- *Known* – Tauren Wells
- *No Longer Slaves* – Bethel Music
- *Who You Say I Am* – Hillsong Worship

FINAL BLESSING

May you always remember that holiness is not a destination but a daily dwelling.
May you find beauty in the spilled coffee, the crooked prayers, and the folded towels.
May you reach again and again for the counter,
And find that grace, joy, and the presence of God are already there.

You were always enough.

FINAL BENEDICTION:
A LETTER TO THE READER

Dear Reader,

You made it!

Not just through fifty-two weeks of devotionals but through fifty-two weeks of life. You showed up in joy, in exhaustion, in laundry-folding weariness, and in quiet, courageous faith. That matters more than you know.

This series was never about reaching the stars. It's about recognizing that grace is already in your kitchen, that beauty is already wrapped into your routines, and that holiness can be found between the crumbs on the counter and the prayers in your breath.

As you step into whatever comes next for you, may you walk not with pressure but with peace. Not with striving but with sacred awareness. Not with a need to prove but with the steady knowledge that you've always been enough.

May your counter continue to be a meeting place of meals and miracles, messes and mercy. And may the God who made you, knows you, and loves you keep showing up in all the most ordinary and extraordinary ways.

With joy and gratitude,
Richard Daniels

ABOUT THE AUTHOR

Richard Daniels is a husband of nearly thirty years and the proud father of three. A lifelong entrepreneur and restaurateur, he brings a practical, grounded perspective and passion to everything he does—whether it's running a business, coaching on the sidelines, or folding laundry on a quiet Sunday afternoon. He's also a dedicated sports enthusiast, a lover of good food, good conversation, and early mornings spent reflecting on life's ordinary, sacred moments.

Richard is a man of faith and gratitude, shaped by his family and inspired by the quiet strength of those around him. His journey as a businessman, father, and husband has taught him to pay attention to the little things—the small acts of love that often go unseen but leave the biggest mark. This is his first devotional, written not from a pulpit but from a lived-in place of observation, love, and appreciation.

He is also the author of *A Tourist in My Own Life: For Fathers Who Yearn for a Deeper Relationship with their Children.*